Praise for *Finding Rest*

"Jon knows better than most what it means to battle anxiety and how to forge a path to victory. He also treats it with care and pushes the conversation to places that it hasn't often gone in the church."

—Kirk Cameron

"A practical, spiritually driven primer on dealing with anxiety, obsessive compulsive disorder, and depression. . . . Excellent advice. . . . [A] cogent, revealing guide."

—*Publishers Weekly*

"Unflinchingly honest, gripping, and full of truth that points readers to our Creator."

—David Ubben, sportswriter with *The Athletic*

"With a graceful balance between practicality and spirituality, Jon shares his story of walking through the dark woods of mental illness yet claiming victory along the way. His honesty blazes the path as he leads us bravely into the most vulnerable parts of anxiety and how we talk about it."

—Hannah Brencher, author of *Fighting Forward* and *Come Matter Here*

"*Finding Rest* is so important. Not only does it give those who are suffering practical tools, but it also gives church leaders the steps they need to take to better support their staff and congregation."

—Holly Tate, senior vice president of growth at Leadr

"[Jon's] stories are incredible, his steps practical, and his takeaways powerful."

—Ben Courson, best-selling author of *Optimisfits* and *Flirting with Darkness*

"In *Finding Rest*, Jon Seidl offers significant help to those suffering from mental health issues and those caring for loved ones who do. . . . Honest, practical, realistic, and full of hope."

—Afshin Ziafat, lead pastor of Providence Church, and council member for The Gospel Coalition

"Everyone will find compassion and great hope, practical power and spiritual inspiration in these pages. You won't be overwhelmed or shamed. In a perfect world, everyone would read this book."

—Dr. Kathy Koch, founder of Celebrate Kids, Inc., and author of *Five to Thrive*

"In Jon, you'll find a kind, empathetic, and humble friend. In the God he leans on, you'll find true rest and help."

—Adam Griffin, coauthor of *Family Discipleship*

FINDING REST

An Invitation to Go Deeper

JONATHON M. SEIDL

KREGEL
PUBLICATIONS

Finding Rest Guiding Workbook: An Invitation to Go Deeper
© 2023 by Jonathon M. Seidl

Published by Kregel Publications, a division of Kregel Inc., 2450 Oak Industrial Dr. NE, Grand Rapids, MI 49505.

The author and publisher are not engaged in rendering medical or psychological services, and this book is not intended as a guide to diagnose or treat medical or psychological problems. If medical, psychological, or other expert assistance is required, the reader should seek the services of a health-care provider or certified counselor.

The persons and events portrayed in this book have been used with permission. To protect the privacy of individuals, some names and identifying details have been changed.

The QR codes provided in this book are included to enhance the reader's interaction with the author and the text. Kregel takes no responsibility for the content accessed by the links and cannot guarantee the links will remain active for the life of this book.

Published in association with Cyle Young of C.Y.L.E (Cyle Young Literary Elite, LLC), a literary agency.

Lyrics to "It Is Well with My Soul" by Horatio Spafford, 1873. Public domain.

ISBN 978-0-8254-4787-7

Printed in the United States of America
23 24 25 26 27 28 29 30 31 32 / 5 4 3 2 1

In memory of Jennifer Lynn Seidl (1984–2018).
I wish I knew then what I do now.
My eyes and ears are open.

"If Jesus is who He says He is, there's another way to look at life. If He's Lord of the storm, then no matter what shape the world is in—or your life is in—you will find Jesus provides all the healing, all the rest, all the power you could possibly want."
—TIM KELLER, *JESUS THE KING*

CONTENTS

FOREWORD

"You are not alone" may be the most potent initial statement someone suffering can hear. Thousands of people have told me their stories of mental and emotional suffering, whether involving anxiety, depression, OCD, or trauma. The average person comes into my office with over a decade of unaddressed impairment. Often that person has anguished in silence for years, not knowing the freedom that is available. Watching facial expressions change from hopeless to hopeful is one of the great joys of my life, and I believe this workbook will accomplish this in many ways.

The *Finding Rest Guiding Workbook* is on the front lines of a shifting epoch in history and the church. Jon Seidl provides a call to action—led by personal example—to see and address mental health as part of the journey of what it means for Christians to love God with their whole heart, soul, mind, and strength.

Can I say in this foreword that I started with skepticism? One might think that someone tasked with writing it is automatically a superfan, ready to sell the book. But I often work with highly complex cases where people feel stuck trying different things. Too often they are hurt because they are given what is supposed to be "the answer" for their mental health, only to continue feeling miserable. Then when they remain stuck, most feel even more shame and isolation. So I was concerned that a brief workbook on mental health would glaringly lack appreciation for the complexity of this profound topic. I was wrong.

Jon continues what he started with his best-selling book, *Finding Rest*, by sharing personal stories of mental illness and recovery. The workbook could be an easy, fast read. But may I suggest taking your time? Move beyond the consumption of words for mere knowledge and allow transformation. Jesus often taught with questions; Jon wields them very well to get to the heart of a matter. You can fill out your answers individually, with another person, or in a group. If you are suffering, I pray for you as I write this, that you will find encouragement as I did. There is surprising depth despite the brevity. Some of my favorite features in this workbook are the ways it

- repeatedly emphasizes a larger purpose and where we fit into it;

- delves into a "proper theology of suffering" that reconciles God's deep love amid the sufferer's substantial pain, with an examination of the life of Job;
- highlights the role and purpose of prayer and offers model prayers;
- discusses the healing power of lament;
- encourages us to trust God and not fall victim to pride, which can hold some back from God's blessings, including medication and therapy;
- thoughtfully addresses the paradox of finding rest *while* experiencing distress;
- emphasizes the life-giving role of community;
- covers the important physical aspects of recovery, such as exercise and nutrition;
- provides consistent guidance for family and friends of the afflicted.

As with most topics in the workbook, concepts are a starting point for further discovery. *Common grace* is an excellent example. Many in the church today feel shame because they think (or are told) they just need to "get over" their struggles or simply "pray about it." Life is multifactorial; so is spiritual growth. In Matthew 5:45, Jesus comments that God "sends rain on the just and on the unjust." These good gifts exist simply because God is love and doesn't require a covenant relationship for people to experience those things. Maybe nowhere is common grace more evident than in mental health. Taking a drink of water, getting sunlight, exercising, or receiving medicine can sometimes go a long way as part of God's blessings for our lives. In other words, let's not despise the little things while holding on to a false god of some immediate fix. The church today often falls prey to "vending machine theology" rather than patiently pursuing God in suffering and utilizing the myriad of good gifts He provides. Common grace and other truths in this book remind us that help often comes from unexpected places and in unexpected ways. Whether through the common or the sacred, God is calling us closer.

Too many Christians try to escape their thoughts and feelings with isolation and guardedness. Mental health requires courage and vulnerability. We who have the hope of the gospel don't have to expect ourselves to have it all together. This mindset is counter to the gospel itself. It is a twisted theology and a spiritual and emotional plague. Sadly, for a follower of Jesus, not having it together is quickly deemed to be a lack of faith. So the person is prone to minimize the problem rather than examine it honestly and deeply while *in* the mess, not just trusting God *after* the mess. This is one of the steps of faith called for in the workbook.

The good news is that God enters into our disorder for us and with us. He does not denounce us for being messy—He meets us where we're at while calling us beyond it. If Christ dives into chaos with love and light, can we follow wherever He goes? This workbook is an excellent way to begin, or to continue, doing this. It is a call that the church needs to heed. While Jon offers some directions for the reader, the open-ended,

Socratic questions help personalize larger truths, as trusting God may involve very different things from person to person. For some, it may mean taking medication. Others will benefit from therapy to learn skills or address the ways they get stuck. Pride often keeps many suffering because of their stubborn refusal to try something different. This workbook can fit into the mix. It does not set itself up as a cure-all—but that is precisely what's so great about *Finding Rest*. "Finding" indicates an active and ongoing pursuit.

God is weaving into His church a movement that can make it the light of the world in the frontier of mental health. The beauty in Jon's approach of *not* offering "the answer" for everything is that he points us to God while also destigmatizing the roles of medication, therapy, support, and all forms of common grace by which God provides for our growth and His glory.

I began reading the workbook skeptical that it could speak to all mental health. I finished it realizing its point is to look to Jesus rather than any other thing we set up in our hearts above God. I believe we will look back in coming decades on Jon's key paving stones of hope in the church for those who suffer mentally and emotionally. He is one of the early voices leading the charge of eliminating stigma and providing hope that our God is for us—not against us—in brain, body, *and* spirit.

> *Trust in the LORD with all your heart,*
> *and do not lean on your own understanding.*
> *In all your ways acknowledge him,*
> *and he will make straight your paths.*
> —PROVERBS 3:5–6

—Justin K. Hughes, MA, LPC

(Scan this QR code for an introductory video.)

INTRODUCTION

To say I'm excited that you're reading this workbook is an understatement. In fact, I'm even more excited that you're reading this than I am that you are reading (or have read) the main book, *Finding Rest: A Survivor's Guide to Navigating the Valleys of Anxiety, Faith, and Life.* (If you haven't picked up a copy yet, be sure to do so.)

Why am I excited? Because if you're reading these words, that means you're the type of person who wants to take action. You want to do more. You're serious about fighting back against your anxiety, your OCD, your depression, or your whatever else. Listen, I'm not saying that those who don't do this workbook don't really want to do the work, don't care, or don't want to fight back. But I can say that if you are here, you are *for sure* the type of person who cares, who wants to do whatever it takes to find rest, and who wants to do the work. And as I say in the book *Finding Rest*, battling your anxiety definitely requires work.

While you can read the book without doing this workbook, my preference is that you do both. Why? Because this guide allows me to go even deeper with you. More importantly, though, it allows *you* to go deeper with yourself.

For starters, in these pages I highlight what I've found to be the most important takeaways from *Finding Rest*. And let me assure you, I am the one making those decisions and writing these words. I know sometimes study guides are written by publishers or ghostwriters. Not this one. It's me. (Hey there!) I think that's important, because it gives you an even greater understanding of what I want you to know, to see, and to meditate on. I don't know about you, but I think that's helpful.

Second, and I think most important, this workbook allows you to get more real with yourself. This isn't your normal stare-into-your-coffee-cup-and-smile type of resource. It's meant to challenge you. It's meant to push you. It's meant to grow you. As I say in the book, I haven't overcome in the past tense, but I am overcoming in the present tense. I'm journeying right along with you. In other words, I'm working on everything in this workbook right along with you. When I challenge you, I'm challenging myself as well. And I'm never going to ask you to do something I'm not willing to do.

We're in this together. We're doing this together. (And if you stick around for the epilogue, which I hope you will, you'll see—in a very vivid way—just how true that is.)

So that's why you'll notice some important words on the front cover. They are intentional: "An invitation to go deeper."

That's what this is, an invitation. The invitation is not to solve all your problems. The invitation is to take what you read in *Finding Rest* and then go further. To explore more. To uncover more. To be heard more. To be more in tune with the One who holds all the answers.

I'm so glad you've accepted that invitation.

So here's what you can expect. First, each lesson of this workbook includes a QR code that takes you to an introductory video. (You'll notice one at the beginning of this introduction as well.) These are especially helpful for group study. After watching the video, turn your attention to the workbook, where I start with a written introduction. This may be a new insight, a doubling down on something from *Finding Rest*, or even a story. In short, it's not just a regurgitation but rather something new, insightful, special, or interesting. I'll then give you key takeaways, turn to Scripture and offer another nugget, and then ask questions I believe are important to discovering truths about yourself as well as the material. Some questions may be short and "easy," while others may be deeper and require more introspection. Regardless, all of them are necessary. I'm not going to waste your time.

You'll also notice a unique section in each chapter for those who may not be struggling themselves but who are supporting those who are. I wanted something for you, too, if you've read the book and are now using the workbook. One of the most consistent pieces of feedback I got regarding *Finding Rest* was how helpful it was for friends and family. So at the end of each lesson, you'll see a question or questions specifically for you, the support system. I'm so glad you're here.

Finally, a few words on the best way to use this resource. First and foremost, it should be used for individual study. That isn't to say group study is not recommended; it is. But this workbook will be most helpful in a group setting if you put in the work on your own first. I hope you do use this in a small group, but that group will only thrive if each member comes prepared.

To that end, here's a suggested rhythm for either an individual or a group setting. For both, I recommend reading *Finding Rest* again even if you have already.

Individual Study

While your time in the workbook may not be as frequent as the group study, I encourage you to make a regular habit of spending time in these pages. To keep yourself accountable, find someone you trust who will hold you to it. Tell them what you're doing and then ask them to text you regularly to see how it's going. In fact, I'd recommend scheduling a consistent check-in time, such as every Tuesday afternoon or every other

Saturday morning. Whatever pace you choose, whether you want to do multiple lessons a week or one lesson a month, it will be good to have the opportunity to unpack what you're learning with someone else.

Group Study

In essence, this is a more regimented individual study with group accountability.

Meeting 1

First, if you haven't already, pick a facilitator who will lead the discussions and then decide together how often you will meet. I recommend weekly, but I also know that may not be possible for everyone. If you don't meet weekly, you'll want to determine how many chapters you want to cover at each session. (If it's weekly or biweekly, I suggest covering only one lesson in order to really get the most out of the study. If it's less frequent than that, feel free to cover multiple lessons at each meeting.)

Once you've determined frequency, at your first meeting be sure to introduce the book and talk about why you're doing the study. Start by going around and having everyone share what they're hoping to get out of the sessions. What are they excited about? What are they afraid of? What do they find particularly challenging right now when it comes to their anxiety and mental health? What have their past experiences been like?

Finally, be clear about the chapter(s) you will discuss at the next meeting. All participants should complete the work on his or her own and come to the next meeting ready to discuss.

Meetings 2+

The facilitator should start each session by asking what stood out to everyone in the group, then work through the questions. You don't have to discuss every question, though. The facilitator should pick out ahead of time which questions seem the most relevant and conversation-inducing. However, each person should have the opportunity to share his or her answers and thoughts for whichever questions the facilitator chooses. If you get through all the questions, great. But that shouldn't be the goal. The goal should be healthy, deep conversations among a growing community.

There are certainly other ways to do the study, and by all means, try them. In fact, email me what works so I can share it with others. This is just the rhythm I've found helpful.

Now that we have all that covered, let's get started. Let's do the work.

CALL IT BY ITS NAME

THERE AREN'T MANY STARS WHO can successfully own a one-name moniker. There's Cher, Bono, and Madonna, sure. But the list isn't a big one. However, that list includes one popular Christian artist: Mandisa.

Even if you don't know her story, you've likely heard the name. Mandisa appeared on the fifth season of *American Idol*, and while she didn't win, she made the finals and left a mark on the competition and the world—especially after publicly forgiving notoriously cantankerous judge Simon Cowell for comments about her weight. She even went on to win a Grammy award for her 2013 album, *Overcomer*.

But a few years later she disappeared from the public eye. Vanished. Gone.

After close friend and former backup singer Lakisha Mitchell died of breast cancer in 2014, partly as a result of choosing to reduce her chemo treatments in order to save her unborn baby, Mandisa went into a deep depression. After losing 120 pounds, she gained about 200 back. She turned to food to cope and found herself suicidal. She became a recluse, venturing out of the house only out of necessity and for McDonald's runs when she got tired of pizza deliveries.

After an intervention from friends a few years later, she finally named what was happening and took control. That culminated in a new album as well as a book on the topic in 2022, *Out of the Dark: My Journey to Find Joy*. It's about grief, abuse, depression, and how friends and family are crucial for healing. It's real, it's vulnerable, and it's necessary.

Why am I telling you this? Because I had a conversation with Mandisa on social media that is extremely relevant to what can happen when we name and take control of our disorder. After the book was released, I came across an interview with her that I found courageous. Instead of running from what happened, she was confronting it head-on.* I posted on Instagram about the interview and thanked her for naming her struggle and talking about it.

She responded. Not just with a customary thank-you but, rather, in great detail about some of her fears related to naming and then writing about her experience.

"Dear Jon," she wrote, "I want to thank you for YOUR words. Since my book came out I've been feeling very vulnerable; like I shared too much. I wondered if it would even matter. Your words reminded me of why I did it. Thank you. In the fight with you, my brother."

I think those words—"I've been feeling very vulnerable; like I shared too much"—are key. They're similar to what I wrote in *Finding Rest*. After explaining for the first time to the world my own mental health struggle, I wondered if *I* had shared too much. I wondered if I was going to be labeled, if I was hurting future job chances, if people would now look at me just a little differently.

Here's what I'm coming to understand after learning about Mandisa's similar struggle: I think many of us go through that. We can recognize in our hearts that talking about our struggles is good and healthy, but there's something in our heads that tells us we've gone too far.

That voice wants to keep us in the dark. That voice wants to control us. That voice wants to tell us we've made a mistake.

That voice is a liar.

Mandisa has found that to be true. I've found it to be true. And if you haven't already, I believe you'll find it to be true as well.

Don't let the lies win. Name what's going on, and then shout it from the rooftops. It loses so much power over you when you do.

Another singer, Francesca Battistelli, puts it well in her song *If We're Honest*. It's a great track you should listen to, but I'll sum it up here. In the opening line, she talks about how telling the truth can be harder than lying. The truth—that we're all a mess—isn't what we naturally gravitate toward. We want to lie, hide, run.

Those things come easy. The lies roll out of our mouths like summer thunderstorms. Hiding feels like second nature. Putting on a front and convincing people we're "doing great" is as common as breathing. But sometimes our worst prison walls are constructed out of the masks we put on and take off every day. The truth? There's something so much better waiting for us when we're honest. If we recognize this and open up, we'd realize we are all messes. And the only way we can get clean—get organized—is by being open and inviting Jesus in.

---

* You can read and listen to that interview: Tré Goins-Phillips, "'I Kept It All Inside': Mandisa Opens Up About Near-Suicide Attempt, Heartbreaking Story Behind 'Overcomer,'" *FaithWire,* March 25, 2022, https://www.faith wire.com/2022/03/25/i-kept-it-all-inside-mandisa-opens-up-about-near-suicide-attempt-heartbreaking-story -behind-overcomer/.

I invite you to do that now, no matter how hard it is. You need that. I need it. We all need it.

What's one practical way you can be open and honest about your struggle? With whom can you share about it?

_____

_____

_____

_____

Key Takeaways
- Naming your struggle gives you power over it.
- The idea of naming something as a form of power is biblical.
- Being vulnerable is a sign of strength, not weakness.

Scripture
Come to me, all who labor and are heavy laden, and I will give you rest. Take my yoke upon you, and learn from me, for I am gentle and lowly in heart, and you will find rest for your souls. For my yoke is easy, and my burden is light. (Matt. 11:28–30)

So what is rest? I've been asked about that a lot. If the book is about "finding rest," then how exactly do *I* define rest? It's a good question, especially because I define rest a little differently than many folks.

The rest I hope you find is not a destination. That may seem counterintuitive, but it's true. When someone asks me what it means to find rest, I tell them it's more like a rest stop than a resort. The fiercest soldier still needs rest while fighting the war. That warrior may do battle multiple times, but between each battle he needs rest. That's the rest I'm talking about. It's rest as respite, and you need it too. Until God takes this struggle completely away, we're going to do battle, and we're going to need to go back to camp and rest up.*

We see that idea in the Scripture above. There's an assumption that we're both doing the work ("take my yoke upon you") while also finding rest ("and you will find rest for your souls"). Jesus was constantly turning things on their head and giving people a new way to look at things (more on that later). I think He's done the same with rest. We find it

---

* Side note: I like to remind people that we wouldn't need the armor of God (Eph. 6:10–18) if we weren't expected to do battle regularly. The armor of God implies that we're going to be doing battle throughout our lives, and it's where this idea of rest as respite was born.

when we put on His yoke, once we take on His burden. And it comes from someone who is "gentle and lowly in heart."

We would be wise to embrace His definition.

How do you define rest today?

_____

_____

_____

_____

How have you historically defined rest amid your battle with anxiety?

_____

_____

_____

_____

_____

Have you found yourself turning to temporal things to give you rest amid your battle (e.g., alcohol, food, TV, people)? If so, list those things.

_____

_____

_____

_____

 Make sure to read the introduction and chapter 1 of _Finding Rest_ before answering the following questions.

Chapter Questions

"Wow! Everything you mentioned in the I Am Second article is me to a T. . . . I've never talked about these things to anyone. I really thought it was just me. My dad is a pastor so a lot of this stuff I feel like I can't share. Thanks for showing me I'm not alone." (_Finding Rest_, p. 18)

Have you experienced shame regarding your struggle? If so, what has that looked like?

How do you think the devil uses shame to keep us bogged down?

> We want to name, and we want to know names. Only then, it seems, can we properly appreciate whatever it is. Only then can we understand it. Only then can we face it. The absence of a name—the unknown—is not only a powerless place but also a place of deep confusion. (*Finding Rest*, p. 27)

Naming something gives us power over it. What are some examples of things you've named in your life—things you have brought into the light even though it may have been hard?

> We didn't talk about it for the rest of the day. In fact, we didn't talk at all. The next morning, she [my wife] expressed how helpless she felt. She was confused and hurt. The term "walking on eggshells" got used a lot as she reminded me this wasn't the first time. There were frustrated tears.
>
> "Jon, your reaction was not normal," she said. She was right. (*Finding Rest*, p. 31)

Make a list of the people in your life who have been affected by your struggle.

Now, write how you think it has affected them. (Maybe they've used some words or phrases to let you know.)

See, owning your diagnosis prevents your diagnosis from owning you. That's what I'm hoping you find in the coming pages. Hope. Hope that you don't have to be controlled by what seems uncontrollable. (*Finding Rest*, p. 35)

If you have named your struggle (or been diagnosed), what did it feel like? If you haven't, what do you feel has held you back from doing so?

Take action

I found freedom when I named what was going on inside of me. A big part of that was talking to others and then seeking professional help. I want you to find someone and talk about what's going on inside of you. That could be a close friend, a pastor, a doctor, a counselor, or a psychiatrist.

Maybe you have done that already; maybe you've sought help. That's great. Keep going. Keep doing it. We sometimes can get complacent once things start going well. That's when we need to be most vigilant.

Pray

(Note: I went through a Bible study a few years back and the leader made a point that is relevant here. We have no problem praying to the Father or Son, but we often neglect the Holy Spirit. And yet the Holy Spirit was specifically sent as our "helper." In fact, when we don't have the words, the Bible says the Spirit "helps us in our weakness" and "intercedes for us with groanings too deep for words" (Rom. 8:26). I don't know about you, but I certainly need that kind of help! So in the prayer examples in this workbook, you'll see me specifically referencing the Holy Spirit every time. I think it's a helpful reminder and exercise.)

Say a prayer asking God to show you the steps you can take to address your struggle, and to give you the courage to actually follow through.

Example:

Holy Spirit, I know the devil uses darkness and secrecy to ensure our struggles rule over us. I ask You to make clear to me daily how I can be open and honest about what I'm going through. Show me the steps I need to take to bring my struggles into the light. Give me the strength to follow through on what You show me. God, show me that You are a faithful Father who honors our obedience and sacrifice. Amen.

For friends and family

What has it been like for you to walk alongside your friend or family member who is struggling? How has it affected you?

_____

_____

_____

_____

_____

If the person you love has named his or her struggle, what was it like when that happened? If your loved one hasn't done so, what do you think is holding that person back?

_____

_____

_____

_____

Write

Use this space to jot down any other thoughts you may have about the introduction and chapter 1.

THE MOST IMPORTANT BOOK OF THE BIBLE

I REMEMBER GROWING UP AND hearing a family member once disparage the sovereignty of God. At the time, my family subscribed to a type of gospel that said you could make God do whatever you wanted if you just prayed hard enough, had enough "faith," and were consistently repenting of your sins.

"The 'sovereignty of God' is just an excuse people use who haven't tapped into the *power* of God," this person said, using those scary and ominous air quotes when saying "sovereignty of God."

How misguided and, frankly, dangerous. The truth is that the sovereignty of God exists, it is true, and it is something we need to embrace. However, that doesn't mean dealing with God's sovereignty is easy. One of the reasons I love the book of Job is because you see so many different emotions from him as he struggles to make sense of what's going on while experiencing God's sovereignty.

There's anger. There's fear. There's confusion. There's depression.

In other words, Job is a great picture of what so many of us have gone through, are going through, and will go through when it comes to doing battle against our disorder(s). I've experienced all of Job's emotions on this journey as well.

But Job's pages are not only filled with a character who is relatable, they're also filled with a foundational truth—a truth so important that I consider Job the most important book of the Bible. That truth is related to God's sovereignty. It's this: God is using all things for our good and His glory.

If there is one thing you need to take from *Finding Rest*, that truth is the thing (and we'll cover more of it later). It's foundational to the book because it's been foundational to me in understanding and dealing with my mental health struggle. I can only find rest when I lean on that truth. The point of Jesus coming is to offer redemption, redemption from the messed-up world that was created when sin entered it.

We are going to suffer in this world. Sin is here. (Thanks, Adam and Eve.) But despite this fallen world, God has promised to use what we go through for our good and His glory. We see that time and time again in the Bible, from Job, to David, to even Jesus.

So hear this: The idea that God is using all our struggles for our good and His glory isn't just some nice-sounding fairy tale we've made up. It's connected to the very essence of the gospel. Through and because of Jesus, redemption is possible—and part of that redemption involves taking our struggles and using them.

Recognizing all of that isn't a cop-out for not tapping into the power of God. God certainly can take away our struggle; He is powerful enough to do that. And sometimes He does. But many times He allows us to remain in a struggle to refine us and redefine us. Friend, that's what your anxiety struggle—or your other mental health struggle—is doing. It's refining you and redefining you.

Too many times we get so caught up in wanting all our hardships to end that we forget that those hardships produce character in us (see Rom. 5:1–5 below). They also produce an appreciation for what God is doing within and around us.

I think we fail to see that so many times because, when it comes to pain, we tend to be animalistic. An animal responds to stimulus—especially pain—in incredible ways. A glorious and powerful horse can be controlled by a tiny metal bit because he can't stand the discomfort it causes in his mouth. The truth is, that horse could overpower its rider at any time, but because of the discomfort it doesn't.

In the same way, pain can be a powerful tool for controlling us. And who do you think does the controlling? Pain is the effect of an evil ruler who wishes us nothing but harm. The beautiful aspect of Jesus is how He takes that and uses it, and then reveals to us that that's exactly what He does.

In his daily devotional called *New Morning Mercies*, Paul Tripp has some of the most brilliant insights regarding this idea in his March 29 entry. I picked out some of the best quotes, but you should read the entire entry when you get the chance:

> Living in this present broken world is designed by God to produce longing, readiness, and hope in me.
>
> It's not natural for us to think about our lives in this way, but the difficulties we all face in this broken world are not in the way of God's plan. No, they are part of it. . . . You are living where you're living and facing what you're facing because that's exactly how God wanted it to be. The hardships that we all face between the "already" and the "not yet" are not a sign of the failure of God's redeeming work, but rather a very important tool of it.

What we are all going through right here, right now is a massive, progressive process of values clarification and heart protection. God is daily employing the brokenness of this present world to clarify your values. Why do you need this? You need it because you struggle in this life to remember what is truly important, that is, what God says is important. . . . So God ordains for us to experience that physical things get old and break. The people in our lives fail us. Relationships sour and become painful. Our physical bodies weaken. Flowers die and food spoils. All of this is meant to teach us that these things are beautiful and enjoyable, but they cannot give us what we all long for—life.

Your Lord knows that even though you are his child, your heart is still prone to wander, so in tender, patient grace he keeps you in a world that teaches you that he alone is worthy of the deepest, most worshipful allegiance of your heart.[*]

Look at it this way: It's because of the darkness that we appreciate the light. It's because of the cold that we appreciate the warmth. It's because of the clouds that we appreciate the sun.

God, in His sovereignty, has made it so that the pain allows us to appreciate the good that much more, to appreciate Him that much more, and to turn our hearts toward Him.

This pain, this struggle, is producing not only character but also appreciation. Don't be so quick to run from it that you miss exactly how God is using it.

I'll leave you with this. I'll chalk it up to a coincidence, although it feels like something bigger than that. In Charles Spurgeon's morning devotion for March 29 (the same day as the entry from Tripp quoted above), he talks about the importance of suffering. Christ suffered, so why should we expect not to do the same?

"Our Master's experience teaches us that suffering is necessary, and the true-born child of God must not, would not, escape it if he could," he writes.[†] Later, he adds another similar insight:

Notice, Christian, that Jesus does not suffer so as to prevent your suffering. He bears a cross, not that you may escape it, but that you may endure it. Christ exempts you from sin, but not from sorrow. Remember that and expect to suffer.[‡]

Maybe instead of trying to run away from the difficult times, we should instead be

---

[*] Paul David Tripp, *New Morning Mercies: A Daily Gospel Devotional* (Wheaton, IL: Crossway, 2014), March 29.

[†] Charles Spurgeon, *Morning and Evening* (Wheaton, IL: Crossway, 2003), March 29, Morning.

[‡] Spurgeon, *Morning and Evening*, April 5, Morning.

thanking God for them. He's using them. He's sovereign like that, and we should rest in His sovereignty.

How has it been hard for you to reconcile your struggles with a good God?

_____

_____

_____

_____

In a few sentences, thank God for what He's doing with those struggles.

_____

_____

_____

_____

Key Takeaways

- God promises to use our struggles for our good and His glory.
- Your mental health struggle is not God punishing you for something you did or didn't do.
- There's a difference between discipline and punishment.

Scripture

Behold, I have refined you, but not as silver;
    I have tried you in the furnace of affliction.
For my own sake, for my own sake, I do it,
    for how should my name be profaned?
    My glory I will not give to another. (Isa. 48:10–11)

I know that you can do all things,
    and that no purpose of yours can be thwarted.
"Who is this that hides counsel without knowledge?"
Therefore I have uttered what I did not understand,
    things too wonderful for me, which I did not know. (Job 42:2–3)

> Therefore, since we have been justified by faith, we have peace with God through our Lord Jesus Christ. Through him we have also obtained access by faith into this grace in which we stand, and we rejoice in hope of the glory of God. Not only that, but we rejoice in our sufferings, knowing that suffering produces endurance, and endurance produces character, and character produces hope, and hope does not put us to shame, because God's love has been poured into our hearts through the Holy Spirit who has been given to us. (Rom. 5:1–5)

> And we know that in all things God works for the good of those who love him, who have been called according to his purpose. (Rom. 8:28 NIV)

I've made no secret of the fact that C. S. Lewis is my favorite author. His story is both incredible and relevant. Growing up he was an atheist, which was driven by the fact that his mother died when he was young, his father was distant at best, he faced immense cruelty from a headmaster when he was young, and he experienced the horrors of World War I, among other things.* In other words, the hurt and pain he experienced as a boy and young man shaped his view of, and approach to, God.

So no wonder he's often quoted as saying, "The problem of pain is atheism's most potent weapon."† But what Lewis came to understand, and what is one of the most fascinating and beautiful aspects of the Christian faith, is that the pain, the hardships, and the downright crap we experience as human beings actually help point us to God.

We are prideful human beings who think we can conquer anything on our own. Our suffering shows us how wrong we are. And while God doesn't cause it, He uses it.‡ He uses it to redeem us and remind us that He is not merely a parachute to be used in times of an emergency (Lewis's analogy) but, rather, the very sustenance we need to survive every day. In this way, the only person ever to be good actually redefines *our* good. We define daily what *we* think good is; God reminds us often how wrong (and selfish) we are. And in His goodness and mercy, He uses the pain we experience to remind us of that, and then shows us that He is not absent in that pain, but very, very present.

That's absolutely beautiful.

This idea, by the way, is not as foreign as we think. It's even worked its way into pop

---

* For a deeper understanding of the life of C. S. Lewis, you'll want to read the 2017 book *From Atheism to Christianity: The Story of C. S. Lewis*, by Concordia University professor Joel D. Heck.
† This quote is likely a summation of his argument in his 1940 classic, *The Problem of Pain*, instead of something he directly said.
‡ I love how Spurgeon puts this in the June 20 morning entry of *Morning and Evening*: "Satan, like a slave, may hold the sieve, hoping for the worst; but the overruling hand of the Master is accomplishing His purpose by the very process that the enemy hopes will be destructive." It's exactly what we see in the death and subsequent resurrection of Jesus.

culture. As someone who grew up in Wisconsin, I'm a country boy at heart. (That's despite living in New York City for seven years of my life.*) As such, I'll often turn on country music, especially on warm days when driving down the road with my truck windows open just feels right. Recently, I heard a song from an artist named Drake White called *Hurts the Healing*. The title is pretty self-explanatory, but I want to unpack it a bit. In essence, White sings about how some of life's greatest struggles—the hurts we experience—are actually steps in our healing. In fact, those hurts have a way of refining us, strengthening us, and creating a resolve within us to finish "this race."

He's absolutely right.

Friend, sometimes God is using temporary hurts for your ultimate healing. It's how He works. It's how He's faithful. And you know what? You don't even have to be the most spiritual person on the planet to see it. You can even be a country singer trying to make the perfect song for a windows-down car ride.

What does it mean to you that God "works for the good of those who love him, who have been called according to his purpose"?

_____

_____

_____

_____

_____

What are some of the hurts you're experiencing in life right now?

_____

_____

_____

_____

 Make sure to read chapter 2 of *Finding Rest* before answering the following questions.

---

* During my time in New York City, I used to joke that one day I was going to dress up in my camouflage bibs and jacket and blow my duck call on the corner of the street to mark the start of the waterfowl hunting season. Funny enough, it probably wouldn't have been the weirdest thing anyone saw that day.

Chapter Questions

In the past, how have you made sense of your mental health struggle?

_____

_____

_____

_____

How would you convey a proper theology of suffering after reading this chapter?

_____

_____

_____

_____

_____

Why is Job so important to understanding a proper theology of suffering?

_____

_____

_____

_____

_____

God's explanation for why He allowed Job to go through all the pain and suffering was: because I am God. His ways are not our ways. He sees the whole picture when we see a fraction of it. It wasn't because of something Job did or because God was angry at him. It was because God had a bigger plan and a bigger purpose in mind. In fact, in Job 1:8 it's *God* who mentions Job to the devil. God is the one who asks the devil if he had noticed Job, thus setting the whole story and chain of events into motion. (*Finding Rest*, p. 42)

Is it hard for you to reconcile that God would allow all this to happen to Job? Why or why not?

_____

_____

_____

_____

Why do you think it's God who brings up Job to the devil in Job 1? What does that say about God?

_____

_____

_____

_____

Job's friends tried to convince him that he had done something to cause his pain and suffering. They were wrong, and God was angry with them for suggesting it. Have you ever heard something from a friend or loved one about your anxiety (or other mental health struggle) that didn't sit right with you? If so, what?

_____

_____

_____

_____

How can we know that our tragedies and our pain are going to be redeemed? Because God tells us that's exactly what He's going to do. My anxiety and your anxiety may be some of the most difficult things we ever experience, but we have hope because God says He's going to use them for our good. (*Finding Rest*, p. 44)

Earlier you listed some of the hurts and struggles in your life. List one way you've seen God use them.

_____

_____

_____

_____

Why do you think we have such a hard time trusting that God will do what He promises He will do?

_____

_____

_____

_____

Too many times we define good as something that makes us feel better, or as the absence of anything bad. We look at Job's restoration and demand that our "good" has to mean a doubling of our possessions, better circumstances, better health, or more money. Or in our instance, no anxiety. But that's not what we see in the Bible. (*Finding Rest*, p. 45)

How have you defined what's good for you in the past? How should you define it going forward?

_____

_____

_____

_____

How do you think your struggle brings God glory?

_____

_____

_____

_____

Our trials have a way of forcing us to admit whether we truly believe what we believe. We can say all we want that "God is enough," but we will never truly know if we believe that until we're forced to live it out. That's why I call Job the most important book of the Bible, because it is a fundamental explanation of who God is and what our relationship to Him should be. (*Finding Rest*, p. 52)

In your own words, write out how your anxiety can help strengthen your faith. If that's hard at this moment, write how you hope to one day view your struggle.

Take action

One of the most important lessons of this book is here in chapter 2: that God is working in your pain and using it for your good and His glory. The quotes from both C. S. Lewis and Charles Spurgeon are powerful. Grab a piece of paper and write down those quotes from pages 51, 52, and 55 of *Finding Rest*. (I've also included them below.) Place them somewhere you will see them throughout the week: on your mirror, on your dashboard, or in your Bible. Meditate on them as often as possible.

Here they are:

God has not been trying an experiment on my faith or love in order to find out their quality. He knew it already. It was I who didn't. In this trial He makes us occupy the dock, the witness box, and the bench all at once. He always knew that my temple was a house of cards. His only way of making me realize the fact was to knock it down. —C. S. Lewis[*]

You will never discover how serious [your belief] was until the stakes are raised horribly high, until you find that you are playing not for counters or for sixpences but for every penny you have in the world. Nothing less will shake a man—or at any rate a man like me—out of his merely verbal thinking and his merely notional beliefs. He has to be knocked silly before he comes to his senses.

---

[*] C. S. Lewis, *A Grief Observed* (New York: HarperCollins, 2001), 52.

Only torture will bring out the truth. Only under torture does he discover it himself. —C. S. Lewis[*]

I have learned to kiss the wave that throws me against the Rock of Ages. —Charles Spurgeon[†]

Pray

Ask God to show you how He is working in the midst of your anxiety or other mental health struggle. But here's the catch: Don't ask Him to take them away. Leave that for another time. Instead, really focus on asking Him to help you understand how He's going to work in the midst of your troubles.

Example:

Dear God, thank You that You are faithful to use my struggles for my good and Your glory. Thank You for what You are teaching me in the midst of them. Holy Spirit, remind me of these truths when I get frustrated, angry, and feel alone. Help me realize that the story You are helping write for me is better than any I could imagine. Make it clear to me how You have been moving in my life even when it's hard for me to see You. Amen.

For friends and family

Looking back, are there some ways you have been like Job's friends? If so, what has that looked like?

_____

_____

_____

Write out some ways you can encourage your loved one to view his or her struggle like Charles Spurgeon, who learned to "kiss the wave that throws me against the Rock of Ages."

_____

_____

_____

---

[*] Lewis, *A Grief Observed*, 38.

[†] I'll clarify Spurgeon's quote here as I did in the book *Finding Rest*. What Charles Spurgeon said in his 1874 sermon "Sin and Grace" was, "The wave of temptation may even wash you higher up upon the Rock of Ages, so that you cling to it with a firmer grip than you have ever done before, and so again where sin abounds, grace will much more abound."

Write

Use this space to jot down any other thoughts you may have about chapter 2.

L E S S O N   3

THE FOUR DEATHS

For most of my life, my family celebrated a cool phenomenon. My stepdad and I share a birthday. That's pretty incredible. It's only topped by another fact: my sister and my stepmom share a birthday as well.

I'm not sure what the odds are that two separate kids share a birthday with two different stepparents, but it has to be pretty low.

And while that was a cause for celebration for much of our lives, it has now become a regrettable reminder of the fact that my sister and stepdad are gone and that death and tragedy are constant companions in this life. My birthday especially has become hard for me because it's simultaneously a day of celebration and a day of mourning.

I tell you that because even though I know the truth that God is using the difficult moments in my life for my good and His glory (like we talked about in the last chapter), that doesn't mean those difficult times won't be, well, difficult.

That's why this chapter is so important. We can say we believe something all we want, but we'll never know it until everything we believe is tested.

That's why those quotes from C. S. Lewis and Charles Spurgeon in the last chapter are so important, and why I asked you to do the exercise related to them. They are the foundation that allows us to weather life's storms, like a sudden death.

That's the point I want to make to you today. The foundation we lay now is what gives us strength in the future.

I learned something interesting when I moved to Texas over a decade ago. There are no basements in much of the South.* That was a shock to me, having grown up in Wisconsin, where basements were the cool areas you built out after the house was finished and served as an entire new level to the home. It's where my friends and I would spend the majority of the time whenever we visited each other's houses.

---

* OK, yes, I'm sure there are *some*, but I don't want any emails about it.

Do you know why there are no basements in much of the South? Because a foundation only needs to go deep enough to get below the freeze line. In the South, like Texas, that's not very deep. In the North, like Wisconsin, it's quite deep.

But here's the thing: Because foundations are not that deep in the South, and because the soil is notoriously full of clay (especially in Texas), the foundations tend to have problems. They crack, they shift, they sink. Several years ago, my wife and I noticed that the walls of our home started forming cracks, our interior doors stopped shutting all the way, and if you put a ball in our front hallway it would roll downhill.

These are all signs of a cracked foundation.

So here's my question to you: Is your foundation solid, or is it cracked? The only way you're going to weather the storms, the only way you're going to survive the freezes in life, is if your foundation is deep, if it's solid.

The deep foundation you and I need is this: God uses our troubles for our good and His glory. Without that bedrock truth, I am unable to deal with any of my struggles, especially the storm of deaths that hit me over the last five years. That's just the truth.

I was recently explaining this to someone and they asked, "So you're saying that your mental health struggle has been harder than dealing with the sudden deaths of your sister and stepdad?" That's exactly what I'm saying. In fact, God used my mental health battle to lay a foundation and prepare me to weather those deaths in a way I could have never imagined. I thank Him for that.

By the way, my wife and I did end up getting our foundation fixed, but it was both invasive and costly. We had to hire a company that dug under our house until they hit super-solid ground. They then inserted concrete pillars, jacked the house up, and finally put it all back together.

Here's the point: If your foundation is cracking, it's still possible to fix it. But the faster you can catch it, the better. Our house was thirty years old. Had we noticed the problem earlier, it would have been easier to fix, less costly, and less invasive.

If you notice some cracks in your foundation, fix them now. Fix them fast. Fix them right.*

Key Takeaways

- It's not enough to say we believe something; the true test of whether we believe it or not is if we hold true to it during the difficult times.
- There's a difference between questioning God and asking God questions.
- It's OK to not understand why something difficult is happening.

---

* When my wife and I built our new house a few years ago, we did something symbolic: we buried a Bible in the foundation. Why? Because we wanted a physical representation of who we are, what we are about, and who is at the core of who we are. Friend, your foundation is crucial.

Scripture

Everyone then who hears these words of mine and does them will be like a wise man who built his house on the rock. And the rain fell, and the floods came, and the winds blew and beat on that house, but it did not fall, because it had been founded on the rock. And everyone who hears these words of mine and does not do them will be like a foolish man who built his house on the sand. And the rain fell, and the floods came, and the winds blew and beat against that house, and it fell, and great was the fall of it. (Matt. 7:24–27)

As he passed by, he saw a man blind from birth. And his disciples asked him, "Rabbi, who sinned, this man or his parents, that he was born blind?" Jesus answered, "It was not that this man sinned, or his parents, but that the works of God might be displayed in him. We must work the works of him who sent me while it is day; night is coming, when no one can work. As long as I am in the world, I am the light of the world." Having said these things, he spit on the ground and made mud with the saliva. Then he anointed the man's eyes with the mud and said to him, "Go, wash in the pool of Siloam" (which means Sent). So he went and washed and came back seeing. (John 9:1–7)

We live in a cause-and-effect world. If I do *X*, then *Y* will happen. Despite our best efforts, then, our relationships tend to become transactional. If you're married, you understand this. The higher the digits in your anniversary number, the greater the tendency is to fall into this trap. Life, kids, jobs, and time have a tendency to turn us into bank tellers dealing in transactions all day.

Is it any surprise, then, that we treat God this way too? That's exactly what is happening in the passage from John 9. The disciples saw someone suffering, and their immediate response was, "Either this man or his parents must have done something wrong to deserve this." They or he did *X* and it caused *Y*.

Jesus, however, turns everything on its head (as He is apt to do). While our life tends to be cause and effect, the beauty of Jesus is that life with Him is anything but. He gave us what we don't deserve and withheld what we deserve the most. Remind yourself of that often, and build your life on *that* foundation.

Too often in the church today, anxiety sufferers are led to believe that they have done something to cause their disorder. How does the above verse from John show that's not the case?

_____

_____

_____

_____

_____

How would you categorize your spiritual foundation today?

_____

_____

_____

_____

What are some examples in your life, currently or in the past, of a cracked foundation?

_____

_____

_____

_____

_____

 Make sure to read chapter 3 of *Finding Rest* before answering the following questions.

Chapter Questions

If you want to understand what you truly believe and if you truly believe it, death, as C. S. Lewis found out, has a way of clarifying those things. (*Finding Rest*, p. 57)

What is one way you have had to practically live out what you say you believe about God?

_____

_____

_____

_____

_____

Have you ever experienced a tragedy that's been hard to make sense of? What was your reaction at the time?

_____

_____

_____

_____

There's a difference between questioning God and asking God questions.

Asking questions is natural, it's normal, and it's expected. But questioning God is something greater, bigger, deeper. In essence it's doubting that He is good, that He is able, that He is capable of turning all these things for my good and His glory. Questioning Him cuts to the core of who He is and who we are. But asking questions in light of Jenny's death in many ways reassured me *more* of who God is, not less, and what He's doing.

Asking the questions brought me closer to Him. Asking the questions reminded me that He is present in our difficulties and our sufferings, in our pain and our diagnoses. (*Finding Rest*, pp. 64–65)

What are some of the questions you've asked as a result of your struggle?

_____

_____

_____

_____

How would you describe the difference between questioning God and asking God questions?

_____

_____

_____

_____

_____

Why do you think it's important to understand the difference between the two?

_____

_____

_____

_____

I haven't gotten an exact answer to all those questions. I may never. But the questions aren't bad. They're healthy. The more I ask them, the more I'm forced to recognize that there is only One who can comfort me, and in asking the questions I am drawn closer to Him. (*Finding Rest*, pp. 65–66)

What hard questions do you want to ask God right now (whether about your struggle or otherwise)?

_____

_____

_____

_____

_____

"The ultimate, best miracle has already happened. It's already secured. Better yet, I actually know Mike is going to be healed. What I don't know is if that healing is going to take place on this side of heaven. But the fact is, he is going to wake up. It's just a matter of if he's going to wake up and see us or wake up and see Jesus." (*Finding Rest*, p. 69)

How can the above quote be a comfort to you in your anxiety or mental health battle?

_____

_____

_____

_____

And I heard a loud voice from the throne saying, "Behold, the dwelling place of God is with man. He will dwell with them, and they will be his people, and God himself will be with them as their God. He will wipe away every tear from their eyes, and death shall be no more, neither shall there be mourning, nor crying, nor pain anymore, for the former things have passed away." (Rev. 21:3–4)

Your battle may not end this side of heaven. How does that truth make you feel right now? Frustrated? Comforted? Confused? Resolved?

_____

_____

_____

_____

What does that mean for your battle today?

_____

_____

_____

_____

If ever I need a reminder that God is not doling out tragedy and struggle as some sort of cosmic retribution, I look at what happened with Mike. Does that mean I'm completely able to make sense of it? No. That's also a lesson the Lord is continuing to teach me. I need to trust Him even when I can't completely figure out what's going on or why it's happening. That's a lesson you can bet is critical to my mental health as I continue this journey. (*Finding Rest*, p. 71)

Have you ever felt like your struggle is punishment? If so, in your own words explain why that isn't true.

_____

_____

_____

_____

Take action

In times of tragedy, we're forced to come to grips with what we really believe. I want you to take a piece of paper and write out in list form all the things you truly believe about God. I'm not asking for the Sunday school answers or the things you think you're supposed to say. I want the real stuff. If you're doing this in a group setting, be sure to discuss with the others what you wrote down. If you're doing this individually, find a trusted friend to talk about the list and why you wrote what you did (and why you might have left some things out).

Pray

Say a prayer asking God questions. Ask Him why you are going through your struggle. Ask Him about past struggles or tragedies. The prayer doesn't have to be long, but make sure to ask, "Why?" Then also be sure to listen and look for ways He might answer that you don't expect.

(Important note: The goal here isn't just to get an answer but to get closer to God through the process. The truth is, an answer may not come right now.)

Example:

> _Jesus, I struggle sometimes with what's going on with me. I need to ask, "Why?" Why do my thoughts go in circles? Why do the little things bother me? Why can't I just be "normal"? Holy Spirit, illuminate the answers, but more importantly, bring me to a closer relationship with Christ through all of this. If answers don't come now or ever, help me be satisfied with what I know to be true already. Amen._

For friends and family

Write out any questions you've asked God regarding why your loved one struggles or why you have struggled as a result of his or her mental health battle.

_____

_____

_____

What is one practical way you can encourage your loved one when he or she is asking God questions or is frustrated with the struggle?

_____

_____

_____

_____

_____

Write

Use this space to jot down any other thoughts you may have about chapter 3.

_____
_____
_____
_____
_____
_____
_____
_____
_____
_____
_____
_____
_____
_____
_____
_____
_____
_____
_____
_____
_____
_____
_____
_____
_____
_____
_____
_____

LESSON 4

THE LITTLE WHITE PILL

I HAD A HUNCH THAT one of the most talked-about aspects of *Finding Rest* would be my thoughts and experience with medication. I was right.

Consistently, the topic of medication came up in interviews and conversations after the book first came out. While people generally responded well to what I had to say, there was something that consistently surfaced even among those who agreed with me. That something was this: *OK, I agree that medication for mental health shouldn't be off limits, but how soon can medication be stopped?*

At one point after publishing the book, I had four separate conversations in one week with people who were taking medication for their mental health that went something like this:

- *I got on meds and they helped me.*
- *But I don't want to be on meds for the rest of my life, so I tried to wean myself off of them.*
- *Once I got off, things were good.*
- *But then something unexpected happened (a death, a stressful event, etc.).*
- *I went into a tailspin and ended up in a very bad place mentally.*
- *Then I tried to get back on my meds and they didn't help fast enough.*

I'm here to tell you that the goal of getting off meds for your mental health is the wrong one. That's not to say I hope you are on them forever, and it's not to say that in an ideal world we would never have to take medication. Rather, what I'm saying is that I don't want you to make an idol of getting off of it. Let me give you an example that will help explain my point.

Not long ago I was looking to purchase a new (to me) truck. Mine had started breaking down. And while I wore it as a badge of courage to drive a paid-off, run-down vehicle and fix it myself, the truth was we had gotten to a point where we were spending more money continually fixing it than if we had something newer and more reliable. At the prompting of my wife, I started looking for an upgrade.*

So one Monday evening we packed up the kids to look at what appeared to be a great deal. However, once we got to the dealership and started going through the process, it became clear the salesperson was pulling a bait-and-switch. The truck that had been advertised for one price mysteriously cost $20,000 more once we saw the paperwork. "Dealer-installed packages," they told us. Never mind that I had talked to several people at the dealership before arriving to confirm the price online was the price we'd pay.

Needless to say, I was frustrated. As my wife drove away in one car and I in another, I decided to stop at a sandwich stop and get us some dinner. I needed a little time to myself to process the aggravation of what had just happened. After grabbing the food and walking out of the restaurant, I strapped in, put my truck in reverse, checked my mirrors and my blind spots, and started backing out. About three-quarters of the way out of the parking spot, I heard a deafening, "Bang!" My heart sank. I turned around to see that a woman driving from right to left had rear-ended me and the truck I was hoping to trade in.

The whole thing happened in seconds. As I stepped out, I could feel myself getting anxious. All the signs of an impending panic attack were there: the heart racing, the frantic thoughts, the quick breathing. It was only heightened once I saw the damage.

But then something happened. I had the presence of mind to take a breath, call my wife, tell her what happened and that I was feeling a panic attack coming on, and then go sit down and wait for the police.

I can't fully explain what a win that was. Yes, a win. Why? Because ten years ago that would have been a debilitating event. I would have had that panic attack. My mind would have been racing uncontrollably. My adrenaline would have been through the roof. I would have entertained all the "What if?" questions that are so unhelpful.

Instead, my wife came, and we talked it through. The police arrived, I swapped insurance info with the other driver (after checking if she was OK), and then we went home.

I believe strongly that if I had not been faithfully taking my medication, the outcome would have been very different. The truth is, up to that point, I had been in a fairly stable mindset for months. But if I had made it a goal to experiment with my anxiety medication—changing the dose or weaning myself off like so many have told me they have tried to do—I'm confident things would have been very different.

Here's my point: I don't take my medication for when things are going well, I take my medication for when things aren't. And what I've learned is that the bad times, the

---

* She got so frustrated with the repairs that one day she said, "Jon, you are in a position that every man dreams of: your wife is begging you to get a new truck. This is a once-in-a-lifetime opportunity, and you're wasting it!" Touché, babe. Touché.

anxiety-producing situations, tend to pop up out of nowhere. If I could plan for them, then they wouldn't really be anxiety-producing situations.

Maybe it's a car accident, maybe it's the death of a family member, maybe it's the sudden loss of a job. Whatever it is, we can't always plan for the things that throw us into a tailspin. And when they happen, it's good to be on our medication so we have a better chance of overcoming them.

Almost two years earlier something similar to my truck accident happened, but on a grander scale.

When I got the call that my stepdad had passed out and was on a ventilator in the hospital, it was tough. It was even tougher when I rushed to Wisconsin to find him completely unresponsive, and it was wrenching being in the room as he entered heaven. However, in the season before I got that call, I was in a good place in relation to my anxiety. So even though it was the height of COVID-19 and I had some anxious episodes, I wasn't nearly as anxious as I could have been. I could have tried weaning myself off my meds that spring. I'm so glad I didn't. The medication in my system that was helping my brain interpret and deal with stressful situations was exactly what I needed.

Can you imagine what would have happened had I gotten that call about my stepdad when I *wasn't* on my meds? I can. And really, it's not that hard to picture, because months earlier I was off my meds for about a month, and Christmas with my wife's family was a disaster. The tiniest of stresses sent me into a tailspin.

John Calvin once said that our hearts are idol factories. We can make an idol out of anything. If the Israelites in the desert could be wearing their gold bracelets one minute and then the next minute make an idol out of them and worship it, you better believe we can make an idol out of getting off medication. And I think that's what a lot of people do. Instead of trusting that God has given us a common grace, we treat it like a poison we need to stop taking as soon as possible.

We can do that with getting off medication, but we can also do it with a lot of other things. In general, we can make an idol out of not being anxious. Is being med-free a good thing to want? Absolutely. In fact, you could make an idol out of being *on* medication.* In the end, anything we elevate above Jesus is an idol.

Friend, there may be a day when you are able to get off medication. But until that day comes, don't play doctor. Don't disparage something God has given to us. Don't make an idol out of getting off your medication and miss what God could be doing with you while you're on it.

And please, be careful while backing out of parking spots. You never know what, or who, is coming around the corner.†

---

* As I've tried to make clear, there is no magic pill. We have to take a multifaceted approach to attacking what's going on inside us.
† The little fender bender had a big twist. A few weeks after it, I got word that despite everyone's claiming at the

How can you protect against not making an idol out of your comfort?

_____

_____

_____

_____

Key Takeaways

- Our mental health is best pictured as a three-legged stool, where the brain, body, and spirit support our overall well-being.
- Medication should be viewed as a common grace from God. A common grace is something God gives to all of us that both helps and blesses us.
- Taking medication for your mental health is not indicative of a lack of faith.

Scripture

[God] makes his sun rise on the evil and on the good, and sends rain on the just and on the unjust. (Matt. 5:45)

No longer drink only water, but use a little wine for the sake of your stomach and your frequent ailments. (1 Tim. 5:23)

I want to be very clear about something: I'm not here trying to play doctor for you.

Remember, I've been very open about what I am not, and I am not a medical professional.

So when I talk about medication, I don't want you to hear that I think every person should be on it. However, I don't think it should be written off, and I do think that Christians in general have been much more hesitant to take it because of misguided views on faith that have wormed their way into our pulpits.[*]

The verse from 1 Timothy above was clarifying for me on this topic. Paul was keenly aware that Timothy struggled with a stomach problem and "frequent ailments." He doesn't tell Timothy to pray more or to have more faith. Instead, he prescribes one of the most common "medicines" of the time.

That's because for centuries the Greeks and Romans used wine to treat a host of

---

scene that they were OK, the person who hit me ended up complaining of a "sore neck" and went to the emergency room. However, once the insurance company determined we shared fault, a settlement came quickly after that. Go figure. Why do I tell you that? Because the incident was even more ripe for producing anxiety. And yet, I was in a much better position to fight against it because I was faithful with my medication.

[*] In the end, this is a decision that needs to be made in chorus with a doctor, counselor, or therapist. Talk about it. Be open to it. Make an informed choice whether or not to take it. Just don't write it off.

diseases, ailments, and even depression.* And while I do not recommend treating depression with wine today, I can look at Paul's advice to Timothy in the context of when it was given and see that Paul himself didn't disparage taking medication but in fact encouraged it.

Thank God for His common graces.

What are some common graces you can think of that God allows all people to experience?

_____

_____

_____

_____

What runs through your mind when you think about Paul's suggestion that Timothy take medication (wine, in this case) for his physical ailments?

_____

_____

_____

_____

 Make sure to read chapter 4 of *Finding Rest* before answering the following questions.

Chapter Questions

What has been your approach when it comes to taking medication for mental health struggles? Why?

_____

_____

_____

_____

---

* Kerry Grens, "Wine Therapy, Middle Ages," *The Scientist*, October 1, 2019, https://www.the-scientist.com/foundations/wine-therapy--middle-ages-66438.

Have you had a hurtful conversation when it comes to taking medication for your mental health struggle? How did you handle it?

_____

_____

_____

_____

_____

Why do you think there has historically been so much shame attached to seeking medical help for anxiety and other mental health issues?

_____

_____

_____

_____

_____

We—those who have struggled with mental health in the church—don't second-guess taking antibiotics for strep throat, but for some reason we were taught to think extra hard about taking medication for our minds. We don't think twice about taking pain medication for a broken ankle, but we hesitate to take it for a broken brain. We take Tylenol for a head*ache*, but we second-guess taking medication for a head *issue*. (*Finding Rest*, p. 81)

Where do you think the hesitation to take medication for mental health issues comes from?

_____

_____

_____

_____

Can God supernaturally heal me of my issues? Of course He can. But what if that's not what He wants for me at this time? For us? And what if He's already offered us some relief? What if He's telling us that He's graced us with a reprieve? Would it not be prideful for us to put a restriction on God and say, "No, Lord, You have to heal me and offer me a way out that I see fit—You have to give it to me on my terms, not Your terms"? (*Finding Rest*, p. 83)

Do you think sometimes it can actually take more faith for us to use medication or seek medical help? Why or why not?

_____

_____

_____

_____

How can completely writing off taking medication for your anxiety be an act of pride?

_____

_____

_____

_____

Even if you are taking medication, there is no "magic pill." What does it look like for you to put in the work while also (possibly) taking medication?

_____

_____

_____

_____

What's one way you can gracefully convey to *others* why we should not immediately write off medication?

_____

_____

_____

_____

(Note: Once again, I'm not saying we all need to be on medication, but rather that we should consider it and not dismiss it.)

Take action

Write a letter to yourself. It doesn't have to be long, but explain why medication for your mental health struggle is a common grace and a valid option to treat your struggle. Maybe you already believe that, but use the points in this chapter to vocalize why. If you don't agree or are on the fence, make a pros-and-cons list and see where it comes out.

Pray

Pray that the understanding of God's common grace would take on new meaning within the faith community, especially as it relates to mental health. Also pray for those who may be hesitant about taking meds, that they would come to a more complete understanding of what God has offered us to help us heal.

Example:

> *Father, thank You for giving us common graces. Thank You for advances in medicine that give us physical tools to fight back in our mental health battle. Holy Spirit, remind me and all of us that You are the giver of good gifts, and reveal those gifts to us in a meaningful way. Amen.*

For friends and family

In this chapter of *Finding Rest*, I talked about a really painful conversation with my mom, who at the time was not happy or supportive of my taking medication. Maybe you've been my mom in this chapter, and you haven't had the best reaction during that type of conversation. What might you say differently now after reading this chapter? If you *have* been supportive, write out how you think you can help others be the same.

_____

_____

_____

_____

_____

Write

Use this space to jot down any other thoughts you may have about chapter 4.

L E S S O N   5

THE PHYSICAL BATTLE

IN *FINDING REST* I TALK about the need for physical exercise to help combat my disorder. Everything I wrote in that section I believe to my core. I have seen how taking care of my body helps me physically, emotionally, and—yes—spiritually. But guess what: After publishing the book I hit my highest weight ever. And my rather short stature magnifies any extra pounds.

Not only did I not recognize myself in pictures, but I felt sluggish; extremely sluggish. In addition, I went through a lot of anxiety and even depression in the months after publication. There are several reasons why that happened (including spiritual attack), but one of them is because, in the busyness of the book launch, I had neglected my physical health.

So in February 2022 I took a big step to reset my physical health. I signed up for a program to help me shed a significant amount of weight. Six months later I hit my goal.

Can I tell you something? The effect that drastically changing my diet, eating right, exercising, and cutting junk food and junk habits from my life has had on my mental health is incredible. It's given me new tools and a new outlook, and I'm not turning to some of those Band-Aid comforts that food provides in times of high stress and anxiety.

In many ways, the program forced me to establish new, healthy habits. Some of those habits are ones I've implemented in the past but had gotten away from.

For example, as I was writing this, I started feeling anxious. I was stuck between whether or not to extend my writing weekend. I hadn't seen my family in days and had two Zoom meetings this particular Sunday evening that had cut into my writing time and productivity. It made sense, then, to stay where I was so I could catch up and double down on making progress. But then my wife would be home alone with our kids even longer and would bear the burden of getting them to school by herself Monday morning. And I would endure another day of missing them all.

I became jittery. I could feel it in my arms, my hands, and my heart.

So what did I do? I made a decision to pursue a healthy habit. I went for a quick run. I got active. While I don't love running, I know it's good for me and that something happens to my anxiety when I run. It helps.*

And it did help in this instance.

After my run, I got clarity. Physically, I was much more at peace. I was much more calm. I was much more . . . restful. I decided to stay. The words flowed even easier in the hours after, and you're reading this now as a result.

Here's what's so encouraging. While the time after first publishing *Finding Rest* was filled with anxiety, I can tell you that prioritizing my physical health in the wake of that season has led to one of the most restful times of my life. And that's in spite of stressful situations. See, because of a slight misunderstanding, I went from having a year to write this workbook to having a month. In any other season of my life, you can bet that would be anxiety-producing! And yet it hasn't been. The stress I expected has been nearly non-existent. My outlook is better. And my mind is clearer. I attribute this to two things: a doubling down in my spiritual life (more on that in the next chapter) and a reprioritiza-tion of my physical health.

Let me be frank with you: Until you take your physical health seriously, you will not experience the rest you crave.† I know for some of you, that's hard to hear. And I'd be lying if I said it hasn't been a struggle for me as well. Up to this point in my life, my physical health has looked like a roller coaster at Six Flags. There have been periods that have been great and other periods that have been, well, awful.

But here's what I can tell you: Whenever my physical health is a priority in my life and is peaking, it makes my mental health battle so much easier. It is only one part of fighting back, true. But it is an important part.

I have never met anyone who decided to get healthier who regretted it. I have never met anyone who decided that taking care of his or her body was the wrong move. It's becoming more and more popular to talk about "doing the work" when it comes to our mental health, and I'm telling you that the physical work you put into taking care of your body and brain is an extremely important aspect of doing that work.

You need that reminder. You need that encouragement. And sometimes you need that kick in the butt. I'm right there with you.

---

* I sometimes jokingly call this "running away from my problems." It's tongue-in-cheek, but it's also kind of true . . . in the best way possible.

† As I talk about in *Finding Rest*, you have to take a multifaceted approach. So my caveat here is, don't do *just* the physical aspect and neglect, say, the spiritual and expect it to be the magic bullet. Everything works in tandem.

Key Takeaways

- Our physical health affects our mental health.
- God has given us physical tools to fight back against our anxiety, tools that we would be wise to take advantage of.
- We need to prioritize finding ways to care for our bodies, which includes everything from eating better to being in physical community.

Scripture

Therefore I tell you, do not be anxious about your life, what you will eat or what you will drink, nor about your body, what you will put on. Is not life more than food, and the body more than clothing? Look at the birds of the air: they neither sow nor reap nor gather into barns, and yet your heavenly Father feeds them. Are you not of more value than they? And which of you by being anxious can add a single hour to his span of life? And why are you anxious about clothing? Consider the lilies of the field, how they grow: they neither toil nor spin, yet I tell you, even Solomon in all his glory was not arrayed like one of these. But if God so clothes the grass of the field, which today is alive and tomorrow is thrown into the oven, will he not much more clothe you, O you of little faith? Therefore do not be anxious, saying, "What shall we eat?" or "What shall we drink?" or "What shall we wear?" For the Gentiles seek after all these things, and your heavenly Father knows that you need them all. But seek first the kingdom of God and his righteousness, and all these things will be added to you.

Therefore do not be anxious about tomorrow, for tomorrow will be anxious for itself. Sufficient for the day is its own trouble. (Matt. 6:25–34)

I need to take some time with you on this passage, because I've come to understand something fascinating, even outside of the mindfulness aspect of these words that I talk about in the book.

First, raise your hand if these verses have ever been used against you. (I'm raising my hand right now.) They make up one of the Bible's classic passages on worry and anxiety, and people who don't struggle like to send it to those of us who do. The insinuation is, "It's easy! Jesus says don't worry or be anxious, so just stop." Or, "Don't you know Jesus tells us not to worry or be anxious? So stop it already!" That's unhelpful.

But as I explain in this chapter of the book *Finding Rest*, there is an aspect of mindfulness at play here that *is* helpful.* Jesus is telling us to slow down, to be more in the moment, to concentrate on today and not tomorrow. Tomorrow has enough worries of

---

* See a more robust explanation of this concept on pages 88–91 of *Finding Rest*.

its own. Thank You, Jesus, for that! But there's also another aspect to this passage that I've come to appreciate.

See, these verses were given by Jesus as part of His famous Sermon on the Mount. And if you look at the Sermon on the Mount, you'll see it's chock-full of Jesus blowing minds on a variety of topics, including love, lust, and divorce. In other words, it's about showing people where they have fallen short, especially when they think they are absolutely nailing it. For example, Jesus says it's not enough to simply avoid adultery; if a man even looks at a woman sideways and with lust, he still has a problem.* The deeper heart issue is still there. Jesus's way of relooking at things is present throughout His sermon.

These verses, then, are Jesus showing us a new way to think. So let's look at *all* that Jesus is saying in this section. It's important to know where His words about worry and anxiety are in the context of what He's saying. They come *right after* Jesus tells us we need to be really conscious about how we treat money. Here is the verse right before it:

> No one can serve two masters, for either he will hate the one and love the other, or he will be devoted to the one and despise the other. You cannot serve God and money. (Matt. 6:24)

And then, the section on worry and anxiety starts with a "therefore." Growing up in the church, I heard this phrase and it bears repeating: "When you see a 'therefore,' you need to ask what the 'therefore' is there for." So let's do that.

Most of the topics covered in Matthew 6 are stand-alones (lust, divorce, prayer). But for some reason, Jesus tells us not to love money and that we can't serve two masters, and *then* He kicks off the next section on anxiety with a "therefore." It seems pretty obvious, then, that the two ideas are connected.

What does that tell us? Let me offer this: Part of what Jesus is connecting here is that we can't be enamored with money and possessions, and "therefore" we need to fight against the anxiety that comes with pursuing them. In short, I think that just maybe He's preaching against how we justify working ourselves to death pursuing more and more money using the excuse "Well, I have to feed and clothe my family, so this is OK" . . . while ignoring that our workaholism has estranged us from our family. Sure, we may have gained the world, and we may have clothed our family, put food on the table, and put a roof over their heads. But we have lost our souls (Mark 8:36).

At a minimum, Jesus is saying our priorities are completely out of whack. But I think it's deeper than that. In the end, He is showing us a better way, a more complete way, a countercultural way. He's telling us to slow down, yes—that's the mindfulness aspect;

---

* Of course, the inverse of this statement is also true for women. Let's not miss the point: adultery is a matter of your heart.

but He's also telling us that we can't justify an out-of-whack pursuit of money and possessions under the guise of "I *need* to do this so we can live." Do we need food, clothes, and shelter? Yes, but not at the expense of making them an idol and losing our souls. When we do, we unsurprisingly become anxious.

I think that's why Jesus asks, "Is not life more than food, and the body more than clothing?" It's an important question that speaks directly to the excuse a lot of family breadwinners give and to how those out-of-whack pursuits affect us.

In case you need more convincing, look at Matthew 6:24–25 without the subject heading break we often see in the Bible after verse 24:*

> No one can serve two masters, for either he will hate the one and love the other, or he will be devoted to the one and despise the other. You cannot serve God and money. Therefore I tell you, do not be anxious about your life, what you will eat or what you will drink, nor about your body, what you will put on. Is not life more than food, and the body more than clothing?

Friend, Jesus came to completely change our thinking and to destroy the excuses we give to chase after everything but Him. The Sermon on the Mount is all about breaking down our attempts to justify ourselves, and Jesus is telling us that those feeble attempts and excuses don't cut it. We pursue money and find a way to justify it, and He's telling us, "No! Don't be so consumed with amassing money under the guise of needing it to survive, and especially not at the expense of what really matters. That pursuit leads to anxiety and worry."

A modern back-and-forth of what Jesus is saying and what He's preaching against may be helpful here:

Us: "I'm not having sex with someone else, so I'm not cheating."

Jesus: "Yeah, but you're looking at him or her lustfully, and that's still destructive. Your heart is still messed up." (Matt. 5:27–30)

Us: "Well, I'm not pursuing money. I'm just trying to put food on the table and a roof over my family's heads."

Jesus: "Yeah, but you're using that as an excuse to chase money because you love it, and it's causing you anxiety."

---

* The chapters, verse numbers, and subheads we see in the Bible weren't used by the biblical authors. They were introduced centuries after the original texts were written.

With Jesus, even the seemingly purest of pursuits can be wrong if done with inappropriate motives. I think that's what we're seeing here.*

So is this passage about anxiety and worry? Absolutely. Does Jesus include a practical tip (mindfulness) for those who find themselves worried and anxious? Definitely. But let's be sure to understand the context and the full message He's giving us. Let's grasp what He's actually preaching against in these verses. He's not beating down those who have clinical anxiety, depression, or OCD and saying, "Just stop worrying already!" He's speaking to those who are putting other things—in this case, the pursuit of wealth—before submission to Him.

That isn't to say we can't be at all concerned with food, drink, or shelter. But there's a difference between being concerned and being consumed. As the *Life Application Study Bible* puts it in the commentary on this verse: "Here is the difference between worry and genuine concern: Worry immobilizes you, but concern moves you to action."†

So when someone sends these verses to you or references them, I encourage you to first give them grace. Not many people view the passage I've described this way. Second, I encourage you to use it for what it's intended to be: a self-check, a litmus test. Ask yourself: Is part of my anxiety on this matter because I've been pursuing something, or some things, at the expense of my soul? Have I made the pursuit of [fill in the blank] an idol in my life, and that's why it's causing these feelings?"

I can tell you from experience that this passage, when used that way, becomes a source of power, not frustration.

What have you traditionally felt when you have read, heard, or been sent the passage above from Matthew?

---

* We see similar words recorded in Luke 12:22–34. There, just like in Matthew, Jesus uses a "therefore" after talking about pursuing money. However, in Luke the point is even more vivid as Jesus uses a parable to talk about "whoever stores up things for themselves but is not rich toward God" (v. 21 NIV).

† *Life Application Study Bible*, 3rd ed. (Carol Stream, IL: Tyndale, 2019), 1598.

How can you implement this passage as a litmus test in your own life?

_____

_____

_____

_____

_____

_____

_____

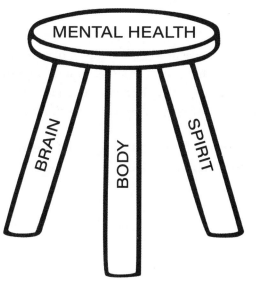

In light of the introductory story as well as the above verse explanation, how would you describe the connection between your brain, your body, and your spirit? (I've included the mental health stool from chapter 4 for your reference.)

_____

_____

_____

_____

_____

Make sure to read chapter 5 of *Finding Rest* before answering the following questions.

Chapter Questions

After reading the chapter, how would you describe the way your physical actions help ease your anxiety?

_____

_____

_____

_____

When I think about [the verse in Matthew above] in terms of mindfulness and consider that, just maybe, Jesus was laying the groundwork for a practical technique I could use centuries later, it gives that verse new meaning and power. It draws me in instead of pushing me away. (*Finding Rest*, p. 91)

When you read Matthew 6:25–34 in light of a sort of spiritual mindfulness, does it help you? If so, how?

_____

_____

_____

_____

Write down how you can put the idea of mindfulness—especially spiritual mindfulness—into practice going forward.

_____

_____

_____

_____

_____

_____

_____

Of the nine physical suggestions listed in this chapter (exercise, fresh air, diet, community, solitude, sleep, serving, hygiene, breaks from phone), which one or ones do you think will be most beneficial to you?

_____

_____

_____

_____

That doesn't mean you're selfish for *experiencing* [mental health struggles], or that you're selfish for talking about them. Not at all. What I mean is that they are inherently self-focused. You are constantly thinking about how this or that will affect you. You're constantly thinking about how *you* feel and how *you* want to feel better. Sound familiar? (*Finding Rest*, p. 98)

Have you ever thought of your anxiety as being selfish (or self-focused)? Does the explanation above make sense to you? Why or why not?

_____

_____

_____

_____

"Studies have found that helping others has tangible benefits, both mental and physical, from lowering your blood pressure to reducing feelings of depression," writes Kayleigh Rogers, who herself struggles with anxiety. "And research hasn't found any significant difference in the types of volunteering—any kind of helpful act can create benefits." (*Finding Rest*, p. 99)

What are some easy ways you can practice serving that can in turn help your anxiety?

_____

_____

_____

_____

Take action

Take a look at your calendar over the next two months. Find an open date, or clear a few hours if necessary. Then find a place you can serve, whether it be a church, a soup kitchen, or a youth club, and do it. Afterward, take note of your attitude. Was it life giving? Did you think about your struggles? How did it make you feel? Write it all down. I think you'll like what you find.

Pray

Pray for follow-through. Taking physical steps can be tiring. Pray for the strength to just take the next step.

Example:

> *God, thank You again that You have given us physical tools to fight this battle—tools like serving. Holy Spirit, I ask You to show me opportunities where I can be Your hands and feet to others. As You illuminate those opportunities for me, give me the fortitude to follow through and the faithfulness to take advantage, even if it is just one small step. Amen.*

For friends and family

One of the suggestions in this chapter is to cut back on our screen time, especially in relation to our phones. How can you model that in your own life? (Be practical.)

_____

_____

_____

_____

_____

Write

Use this space to jot down any other thoughts you may have about chapter 5.

LESSON 6

THE SPIRITUAL BATTLE

I still can't believe I lied. It was so silly.

In addition to writing, I lead a digital media consulting and content creation business that I founded. It allows me to use my experience to help people, while being flexible enough to write and talk about the things (like this) that matter most.

Recently, I wanted to send a gift to a very important client whom I had partnered with on a big project. I asked his assistant what he liked, and she gave me the name of a wine and a bourbon that he really enjoyed.

Because this client is what you would call a "high roller," the wine and bourbon were slightly exclusive. So I proceeded to drive around the Dallas–Fort Worth metroplex to locate them. I finally found both of them at a small, locally owned shop. I bought them as fast as I could, brought them home, and packed them in a box to ship them out.

There was just one problem: Apparently you can't ship alcohol. But I would find that out the hard way.

I had done some research about shipping wine and spirits, but I didn't pay close enough attention. I thought it was kind of a gray area. I had also known plenty of people who had done it, including a friend who recently sent my wife and me a bottle of champagne.

"I'll take a chance," I told myself.

Bad idea.

On my way out of town one Friday, I stopped at the UPS Store to send the gift. I walked in and set the box on the scale. Now, you should know that I packed this box really well, with large sheets of bubble wrap around each bottle. At the bottom of the box I put Styrofoam. On the top I put those giant, plastic air packets you get with Amazon packages. This stuff wasn't going to break!

As I started doing the paperwork, the young man at the counter asked me what I was shipping.

"Business gifts," I said. "Glass business gifts."

I was being coy. I knew it was a (supposed) gray area, and I also knew I had spent a pretty penny on this wine and bourbon and didn't want my package to go "missing" once he heard what it was.*

So I told a half-truth. But that half-truth soon turned into a full lie.

"OK, but what exactly are the gifts?" the young man asked.

I froze a little bit as I searched for what to say.

Should I just tell him?

What if he steals the contents?

What if he doesn't accept it?

So I did something I'm really not proud of. I lied.

"Ummm, glass . . . vases," I said quickly. By the time I said it, it was too late to take back. He typed it in his computer, gave me the total shipping cost, and then sent me on my way.

I didn't feel great about lying, but I told myself that it was justified. *It's not a big deal.*

Three days later, though, I got a call.

"Mr. Seidl, this is Jake from the UPS Store; do you have a minute?"

"Uhhh, yes," I said, somewhat sheepishly.

"Sir, I'm calling to tell you that your most recent shipment was damaged in transit. As a result, the contents broke. When that happened, it became clear that there was alcohol in the box. The contents were discarded. However, I need to let you know that it is illegal to ship alcohol, and it looks like you told our associate—let me check here—that these were business gifts consisting of glass vases."

I was caught. I was embarrassed. I was ashamed.

"I'm so sorry," I said. "I didn't fully realize it was actually illegal. I thought it was more of a gray area."

But then it got worse. I felt so ashamed about the "vase" lie that I dug myself a bigger hole.

"But I'm not sure I told your associate they were vases. I thought I just said it was filled with glass business gifts," I said.

I'm blushing just retelling this.

The person, who I'm assuming was the manager, brushed it off and told me that if I

---

* Interestingly enough, a month later I was trading in an old iPhone and told the associate at a rival shipping store what was inside. The phone never made it to Apple. The box did, but not the phone. Apple determined it had been tampered with and the phone stolen in transit.

wanted to ship alcohol in the future, I'd have to apply for a certain permit. I told him I understood, and we hung up.

I got off the phone, and my anxiety shot up even higher than before. Why? Because I knew that not only did I get caught in a lie, but I had told another one.

Who am I? I asked myself. *Who does that?*

I spent the next twenty-four hours doing some soul searching. I didn't like how easily those two lies came out of my mouth. I didn't like how I felt afterward. And I didn't like what all that said about me.

In my searching, I realized something important: I had recently been neglecting my spiritual exercises.

I say in *Finding Rest* that many people will ask which is more important, the physical battle or the spiritual battle. My response: It depends on where you find yourself deficient at the time. Leading up to this incident, my physical health had been the best it had been in years. I was exercising regularly, eating right, and shedding excess weight.

My spiritual life? That's another story. I hadn't been giving it the care and attention it deserves. I was cutting corners—sleeping in a little longer and foregoing starting my day with the spiritual practices I know I need, watching church online because, well, it was easier.*

This was not my proudest moment. But in some ways, it's not surprising. Friend, I try to be really clear about who I am. And while it has become cliché to say, "I'm not perfect," clichés tend to be clichés because they're true.

Every day I'm more and more aware of my faults, my shortcomings, and my tendency toward sin. And while I'm better than I was, I'm not who I want to be. Part of becoming older, wiser, and more like Jesus isn't that we're always going to make the right and best decisions, but rather that we're much more keenly aware of when we fall short.†

I fall short.

And one way I've fallen short is that leading up to this point, I had neglected my spiritual life.

Why do I tell you that? Because I'm going to guess you've been here too. And you will be here again. When that happens, look for the little signs that will help you see it.

For me, one of those signs was how easy it was for me to lie. This whole series of events reminded me not only how much I had been neglecting my spiritual battle but also how much I needed to refocus on it.

---

* Let me be clear: Not having a regimented "quiet time" or watching church online instead of going aren't sins, and they don't make you a bad person. (We're already bad on a fundamental level, which is why we need Jesus.) I just know that these are two things that *for me* are some of the first steps in feeling disconnected from God and for me are the antithesis of investing in my spiritual life. That disconnectedness may look different for you.

† However, the more we pursue Jesus, the more and more our actions are transformed, not out of fear but out of respect and obedience that the Holy Spirit pushes us toward.

That's where I had been most deficient. And with that realization in mind, it became easy to see why my mental health had taken a hit as well.

So let me ask you: How are you doing in your spiritual battle lately? It's better to consider that question now before you end up in a sequence of lies you can't take back.

Key Takeaways
- When it comes to which issues are most important in your life, the physical or the spiritual, it comes down to where you are most deficient in the moment.
- Spiritual disciplines are essential to growing us, shaping us, and helping us in our mental health battle.
- Our anxiety lies to us constantly, and ultimately it manifests as a pride issue. It tells us *we* can control everything, *we* can figure everything out, if *we* just try harder.

Scripture
For we do not wrestle against flesh and blood, but against the rulers, against the authorities, against the cosmic powers over this present darkness, against the spiritual forces of evil in the heavenly places. (Eph. 6:12)

We are prone to pendulum swings in life. In my own life I can go from one extreme to the other. I've referenced my upbringing a lot in *Finding Rest* as well as a bit in these pages, but it's important here as well. That's because for most of my young life, I was led to believe that a lot of my struggles were purely spiritual. The hurts, the pains, or the lack of whatever were because my spiritual life wasn't up to snuff.

Then for much of my twenties, I swung the pendulum toward downplaying the spiritual, especially spiritual warfare—the idea that we suffer attacks consistently from the devil and that he's out to get us. It's not that I didn't believe in it, but I was more apt to dismiss the bad things with temporal explanations. And while I still think some people are quick to make everything spiritual (think about the person who loves to talk about God's giving her a great parking spot, or who chalks his job loss up to the devil instead of examining his own lack of productivity and follow-through), I've found that I need to do better at recognizing spiritual attacks.

For example, I experienced a panic attack and a depressive episode just two weeks before *Finding Rest* was released. That's not a coincidence. It was, well, an attack. Just like I don't want to downplay the physical, I also have to guard against downplaying the spiritual.

Friend, "the devil prowls around like a roaring lion, seeking someone to devour" (1 Peter 5:8), and "comes only to steal and kill and destroy" (John 10:10). Let us not forget that, and let us prepare ourselves spiritually to repel those attacks.

Do you find it difficult to consider that your anxiety is both a physical and a spiritual issue? Why or why not?

_____

_____

_____

_____

_____

What is one way this week you can prepare yourself spiritually for the devil's attacks?

_____

_____

_____

_____

 Make sure to read chapter 6 of *Finding Rest* before answering the following questions.

Chapter Questions

The natural questions I'm sure you're asking (because I've asked them myself) are: "So which aspect is more important, the physical (brain and body) or the spiritual? Where do I start? What deserves more attention?" Those are not bad questions, but I think they are the wrong ones.

The better question is: where am I currently most deficient? (*Finding Rest*, p. 104)

Think about where you are currently in your anxiety battle. If you had to name the area where you are currently most deficient, would you choose physical or spiritual? Why?

_____

_____

_____

_____

For me, addressing my disorder in a physical way (medication plus what I mentioned in the previous chapter) puts me in a position where I am able to address, face, and attack the roots of what is going on within me. It gives me the best chance to address the deeper spiritual issues, which feed what's going on in my brain. (*Finding Rest*, p. 106)

What would you say are the spiritual issues at the root of your personal anxiety struggle right now?

_____

_____

_____

_____

_____

_____

_____

We may say we believe God is all-powerful and all-knowing, but then we don't act like it. (*Finding Rest*, p. 107)

What is one way you haven't acted like God is all-powerful and all-knowing?

_____

_____

_____

_____

_____

_____

The idea is that if we live like we believe He loves us, our lives would be radically different. It's true. So many of my own sin struggles can be traced back to either not really believing God loves me and cares about me or at least not internalizing it. (*Finding Rest*, p. 108)

How would you live differently if you truly and fully believed God loves you?

_____

_____

_____

_____

_____

When we either doubt God's abilities or doubt His love for us, we then feel a need to step in, to take control, to try to fix things and make them go our way. Rarely does that work out. (*Finding Rest*, p. 109)

How does your anxiety try to be like God?

_____

_____

_____

_____

_____

When we step in and try to take control, not surprisingly we get overwhelmed. That, in turn, leads to more anxiety. It's a vicious cycle. Since our gazes are turned inward, we frantically look for things to give us instant relief. Sound familiar? (*Finding Rest*, p. 110)

What are some of the physical things you have used to numb the effects of your anxiety?

_____

_____

_____

_____

_____

In this chapter, I lay out three spiritual disciplines that can help us address the spiritual roots of our anxiety. Of the three mentioned (meditation, prayer, study), which one do you feel you should particularly focus on going forward? Why?

_____
_____
_____
_____
_____
_____

> For much of my life I have treated prayer, or what it can give me, as the end instead of the means. But that couldn't be further from what prayer is meant to be. Prayer is a conversation. It's our primary means through which we cultivate a relationship with the One who can give us rest. It doesn't have to be this stuffy, highly regulated practice that we should fear. (*Finding Rest*, p. 115)

How have you traditionally viewed and approached prayer?

_____
_____
_____
_____
_____

When we view prayer as being not about what we can get but about how it brings us closer to God, how does that help you in your struggle?

_____
_____
_____
_____

What's one practical way this week that you can prioritize your prayer life?

_____

_____

_____

_____

What you watch affects you. In fact, studies have shown that an increase in watching cable TV lowers your IQ. If that's what it can do to your brain, can you imagine what it can do to your spirit? (*Finding Rest*, p. 118)

How have you seen in your own life how what you watch, or even read or listen to, affects you?

_____

_____

_____

_____

But hopefully you've seen how mental health and spirituality are connected and how, when approached correctly, their interconnectedness is not something to run from but something to press into. (*Finding Rest*, p. 119)

After reading this chapter, how would you describe how your mental health and spiritual life are connected?

_____

_____

_____

_____

Take action

Earlier, you wrote down one of the three spiritual disciplines that you'd like to work on. Now put it into practice. Really focus on it this week and see what happens. Record your experience on the following page or your notes app on your phone. Pay close attention to what practicing the discipline does to your outlook on life, your mental health, and your relationships.

Pray

Pray that God would reveal to you the root issues at the heart of your anxiety.
Example:

> *Dear God, I know I am not perfect. I know that while there are real physical issues contributing to my anxiety, there are also deeper heart issues. Holy Spirit, illuminate those issues for me. Show me where I have been lacking and what I have to root out, and then give me the strength to do the work required. Amen.*

For friends and family

Sometimes an outsider's perspective is extremely helpful for someone struggling with anxiety. When you look at what your loved one is going through, where do you think he or she can make the most improvement spiritually?
(Note: This isn't an excuse to bash that person over the head but, rather, an opportunity to provide an objective look.)

_____

_____

_____

_____

_____

Write

Use this space to jot down any other thoughts that you may have about chapter 6.

_____

_____

_____

_____

_____

_____

_____

_____

_____

_____

_____

_____

_____

_____

_____

_____

_____

_____

_____

_____

_____

_____

_____

_____

_____

LESSON 7

A PRESCRIPTION FOR THE CHURCH

I WALKED INTO THE RESTAURANT and headed for the back party room. That's where Ben immediately caught my eye. Even though he was much taller than me—well over six feet, while I'm five foot six—it was like looking in a mirror. We both sported a shaved-head look, with just over a five o'clock shadow on our faces. We both had dark-rimmed, plastic glasses. We had both put on "the COVID 19" around our midsections. And we both were (and still are) gregarious and jovial.[*]

I wasn't the only one who noticed. As I looked for a place to take a seat at the business dinner we were attending, nearly everyone there called out the similarities. We both laughed and decided to embrace the coincidence. As a result, I picked a chair across from him.

At the time, Ben and I were both working as consultants for the same company. The CEO had invited us to a team-building dinner at a local steakhouse. While I didn't know it at the time, that dinner would be the start of one of the most enriching friendships of my life.[†]

From that moment, something special blossomed. We began talking on the phone regularly, and we found that we viewed the world, God, movies, and a slew of other things the same. In fact, for almost a year straight we talked on the phone every weekday

---

[*] We're also louder, although I take that to another level. I constantly find myself on the receiving end of a "Shhhh!" or other exclamation about my voice. By this point, I've just embraced it. It's who I am. And it isn't a coincidence that my son has followed in my footsteps. More is caught than taught, as they say.

[†] It almost didn't happen, though. In college, there was a similar person whom others predicted would become my best friend. He didn't, despite its seeming like a perfect pairing. That jaded me a little. So when others started whispering that Ben and I were so similar we were destined for a deep friendship, I approached it with a lot of trepidation and even initially resisted. Once we started talking, though, our connection was unavoidable.

morning, sometimes going deep while other times joking and just catching up about the previous day.

As we cultivated our friendship, something started happening. When you talk to someone every day, you inevitably share your struggles. As those struggles popped up, we found each other speaking into them. I would give Ben thoughts and advice on what he was going through, and he would give me thoughts and advice on what I was going through. When I had a panic attack just before *Finding Rest* was released, Ben was the friend who talked me through it and reminded me of the things I knew to be true.

Here's the thing, though: His advice wasn't always what I wanted to hear, and my advice wasn't always what he wanted to hear. But you know what? That was OK. Why? Because both of us had earned the right to speak into the other's life. When friendship, familiarity, and relationship are present, tough conversations, tough advice, and tough words are much sweeter and much more palatable.

I remember one conversation in particular. I had recently made a realization after some searching: Despite my willingness to be open and honest in my writing, there were some relationships that had become much more transactional. I had been holding back, only going surface-level and being more concerned with what I could get out of the relationship in order to achieve some predetermined end.

During a retreat, Ben and I took to the woods, and I opened up to him about my discovery.

"I know," he said.

"You know?" I asked. I got nervous. Was he feeling I had been doing that with him?

"I don't think it's happened with us, but I could tell early on that you can fall into that trap," he responded. I was shocked. I thought I hid it so well. Those comments were the start of a deeper conversation, a conversation in which Ben challenged me and offered advice on how to combat that tendency.

That conversation is a perfect example of what I talk about in this chapter of *Finding Rest*. If Ben would have begun our relationship by calling out this shortcoming of mine, I'm not sure it would have gone well. But because his input came after we had established a deep relationship, I wasn't only receptive but eager to hear his thoughts, and I welcomed his challenges.

That's not the only time Ben and I had tough conversations. Remember when I admitted earlier in this workbook that I lied to the UPS man? Well, shortly after that happened I told Ben about it. In order to make myself feel better, I told it to him in a half-joking, can-you-believe-what-happened manner. You know what he told me?

"You crossed the line there." Now, he said it with a chuckle, but the message was clear: I wasn't getting away with playing it down. It was wrong, and he let me know it. And I am so grateful he did.

We need more of that in the church today. "That" is truth telling that comes after deep, trusting, and loving relationships have been established. What we need less of is the attitude that we are all Old Testament judges and prophets called by God to stand on a street corner with a bullhorn or a sign and call out anyone within earshot. In this age of social media especially, we get so preoccupied with smashing people over the head with the truth that we forget about the love-and-grace aspect that actually makes our words stick. As an anxiety sufferer, you've likely experienced that. You've probably had people you barely know throw Scriptures about rest and peace at you. And not only has it been unhelpful, but it has probably alienated you.

Are there times when it's right and necessary to call out gross examples of sin? Of course. But I'd love to see our default become more about building relationships first. Because when we do, the truth in those conversations is better received, better heard, and better practiced.

If I'm wrong, I fully expect Ben to call me out about it. He's earned that right.[*]

Key Takeaways
- The church—no matter the denomination—has historically treated mental health as *only* a spiritual issue. It is not.
- The church can serve anxiety sufferers better by teaching both the ideas of lamenting and a proper theology of suffering, as well as engaging in meaningful relationships with those who are struggling.
- A proper theology of suffering judges our circumstances by who we know God is instead of judging God by our circumstances.

Scripture
How long, O LORD? Will you forget me forever?
   How long will you hide your face from me?
How long must I take counsel in my soul
   and have sorrow in my heart all the day?
How long shall my enemy be exalted over me?

Consider and answer me, O LORD my God;

---

[*] I do want to add a caveat: While I believe strongly that relationships are vital for speaking into each other's lives knowledgeably and lovingly, that doesn't mean we all can't get better at receiving hard feedback from all kinds of people, sometimes even strangers. We anxiety sufferers don't get a free pass to be offended all the time. Both things can be true: people giving feedback need to do better at cultivating deeper relationships beforehand, and people receiving feedback need to do better at giving people the benefit of the doubt and not automatically becoming defensive. I've especially seen how necessary this is in marriage.

light up my eyes, lest I sleep the sleep of death,
lest my enemy say, "I have prevailed over him,"
    lest my foes rejoice because I am shaken.

But I have trusted in your steadfast love;
    my heart shall rejoice in your salvation.
I will sing to the LORD,
    because he has dealt bountifully with me. (Ps. 13)

My God, my God, why have you forsaken me?
    Why are you so far from saving me, from the words of my groaning?
    (Ps. 22:1)

About the ninth hour Jesus cried out with a loud voice, saying, "Eli, Eli, lema sabachthani?" that is, "My God, my God, why have you forsaken me?" (Matt. 27:46)

Can you imagine the physical pain and emotional abandonment Jesus felt on the cross? I know in my head it happened, but I don't think I fully understand the level of anguish associated with all that went on.

Jesus was physically beaten beyond recognition, and on top of that, He had to experience the abandonment of the Father, all to reconcile us with God. When that happened, what did Jesus do? He lamented. That should be a signal to us about the power and necessity of lamenting.

At our weakest moments, in those moments when we can't make sense of everything, when maybe we know the right answers but struggle to embrace them, we can lament. We can cry out to God, asking Him our soul's passionate questions. And when we do, there's something that happens. He comes closer.

Not just if but when you find yourself at one of those moments, follow the example of Jesus: lament, and wait for God to respond to your cries by drawing closer to you.

When you think of Jesus lamenting on the cross, what visual images come to mind?

_____

_____

_____

_____

How can David's laments in the Psalms comfort you?

_____

_____

_____

_____

 Make sure to read chapter 7 of *Finding Rest* before answering the following questions.

Chapter Questions

What has your experience been with the church as it relates to your mental health struggle?

_____

_____

_____

_____

This type of thinking reduces God to a vending machine: if I put in the correct change, I can pick what He gives me—good health, lots of money, success, and the like. (*Finding Rest*, p. 125)

What are some ways you've treated God like a vending machine in the past?

_____

_____

_____

_____

What effect do you think that's had on how you've approached God?

_____

_____

_____

_____

How do you think it has affected the way you've approached your mental health?

_____

_____

_____

_____

_____

> I am convinced that unless someone battling mental health has a proper understanding of prayer and specifically prayers of lament, that person will never find rest. Yet many churches rarely preach lament. (*Finding Rest*, p. 127)

How would you explain to someone what lamenting is?

_____

_____

_____

_____

How does it encourage you knowing that Jesus quoted David and lamented on the cross even though He knew He was in line for ultimate victory?

_____

_____

_____

_____

> "He [David] chose to interpret his circumstances by God's love rather than to interpret God's love by his circumstances."* (*Finding Rest*, p. 130)

---

* Steven J. Cole, "Psalm 13: When God Seems Distant," Bible.org, 1993, https://bible.org/seriespage/psalm-13-when-god-seems-distant.

How have you interpreted God's love by your circumstances instead of the other way around?

How do you think you can encourage the global church to do even more for people who are struggling with mental health battles?

One of the biggest issues I see is that people pretend everything is perfect. They project an image that is far from reality. You know what breaks down those walls? The wrecking ball of weakness. So the more the church cultivates an environment where it's OK to talk about our struggles—all of them, not just the ones people tend to be comfortable with—the more those struggles lose power over us. (*Finding Rest*, p. 134)

How have you put on a mask regarding your struggles in the past?

What are some good ways you've seen Christians and the church handle mental health?

Take action

Maybe you attend a church that handles mental health well. That's great! Find a way to say thank you to your church leaders, and tell them how much their support means to you. However, if you feel like your church could do more, I encourage you to have a conversation with someone who could help bring about change. Maybe that's the pastor or a pastoral care minister. You could even give that person a copy of *Finding Rest*. But this is important: Do it with a posture of humility. Don't bash anyone over the head; rather, gently show church leaders a better way.

Pray

Pray that both the local church and the global church would recognize how they can better serve those who suffer from anxiety and other mental health concerns. Also pray that any conversations you have about this topic would be grace-filled, full of humility, and productive.

Example:

> *Dear God, thank You for giving us community, even though it can sometimes be messy. Thank You for giving us the church, a group of imperfect human beings trying to be more like You. Jesus, I pray You would help Your church be better at ministering to those of us with mental health issues. Holy Spirit, give our leaders a deeper understanding of these issues, and draw us together as we pursue You. Give me the humility to approach any wrongs, perceived or otherwise, with grace and demonstrate who You are as I have these important conversations. Amen.*

For friends and family

What would it look like for you to be an advocate for your loved one, especially as it relates to calling the global church to be better at serving mental health sufferers?

_____

_____

_____

_____

_____

Write

Use this space to jot down any other thoughts that you may have about chapter 7.

LESSON 8

AN ONGOING BATTLE

I'm a hypocrite.

Let me just put that out there. If anyone were to name things in my past that I've done wrong, I would most likely agree. There are things I've done and said that I'm not proud of and moments I wish I could take back. There are ways I've coped with my disorder in the past that I see now were destructive.

There are snapshots of my life you could show me and say, "Jon, you're not following your own advice." I would agree. And I've accepted that.*

For years, though, I would beat myself up over my past mistakes. As someone with OCD, I can be haunted by my past more than most people. In fact, I can still replay unkind words I said to classmates in middle school and get a sinking feeling in my stomach. I shudder thinking about moments in the past when I did not live out what I claim to believe and failed to demonstrate Christ.

All that is why I'm so thankful I came to understand the process of *sanctification*. Growing up, I had never heard of this word or concept. But in college I was introduced to it, and in early adulthood I came to really understand it.

Sanctification, at its core, is the idea that we are progressively being made holy. As that process continues, we are becoming more and more like Christ. That means we may look at things we did fifteen, ten, or even two years ago with a cringe.

In other words, it's saying, "I'm not where I was yesterday, and I'm not where I will be tomorrow."

It's a process.

So why do I bring that up? Because the ongoing battle against my disorder makes much more sense when I consider sanctification. Jesus is constantly drawing me to

---

* Still, accepting it does not mean I can use it as an excuse to not work at being better. Romans 6:1–4 makes that clear. My love for Jesus should prompt a response and desire to follow what He says.

Himself. He is refining me. He's redefining me. He's giving me new words, new perspectives, new loves. He's growing within me a distaste for who I was yesterday and a striving for who I will become in Him tomorrow.

All those things can be applied to my anxiety. Ten years ago I handled my anxiety much worse than I do today. And ten years from now I will handle it much better than I do today. That's because as God continues to draw me to Himself, and as I pursue Him more, I am formed more into His image.

And that process can be really messy.

On this journey, if you haven't done so already, you're going to feel like you've blown it. You're going to feel like you're a hypocrite. Guess what: You *have* blown it. You *are* a hypocrite. I'm a hypocrite. We're all hypocrites. It's why we need Jesus. Daily.

"The fact of the matter is that none of us are grace graduates, including the man who is writing this devotion," Paul Tripp writes in *New Morning Mercies*. "We are all in daily and desperate need of forgiving, rescuing, transforming, and delivering grace."[*]

Me, you, him, your friend, your family, your pastor . . . all of us need grace.

Tripp goes on: "This work of rescue is not yet complete in any of us. Yes, by grace we love the world less than we once did and we surely love God more than before, but our hearts are still torn and our loyalties at points are still confused. But we need not fret, because grace will win and bring final rest to our worship and our love."[†]

Grace will win and bring *final* rest. Grace. Jesus has given it to you; now give it to yourself. You are a work in progress. Accept that, live in its freedom, and keep going.

Key Takeaways

- You will fail. You will mess up. You will get knocked down, sometimes during unexpected as well as expected battles. And you will realize how much you need Jesus as a result.
- Anxiety can be boiled down to the tyranny of the "What if?"—the ever-present question we ask ourselves that leads us to entertain worst-case scenarios.
- As you face your battle, it can help to focus on the smaller picture—the immediate next steps—instead of getting caught up in the bigger picture.

Scripture

So to keep me from becoming conceited because of the surpassing greatness of the revelations, a thorn was given me in the flesh, a messenger of Satan to harass me, to keep me from becoming conceited. Three times I pleaded with the Lord about this, that it should leave me. But he said to me, "My grace is

---

[*] Paul David Tripp, *New Morning Mercies: A Daily Gospel Devotional* (Wheaton, IL: Crossway, 2014), March 30.
[†] Tripp, *New Morning Mercies*, April 5.

sufficient for you, for my power is made perfect in weakness." Therefore I will boast all the more gladly of my weaknesses, so that the power of Christ may rest upon me. For the sake of Christ, then, I am content with weaknesses, insults, hardships, persecutions, and calamities. For when I am weak, then I am strong. (2 Cor. 12:7–10)

If you spend just a little time in the mental health community, you'll hear a phrase: "It's OK to not be OK."* I love this phrase. It's true, it's encouraging, and it's freeing. At its heart, it's about being honest and open and, in a sense, boasting about our weaknesses like the Scripture above describes. I'm a huge advocate of all those things. But I think it's a phrase that needs to be accompanied (not necessarily replaced) by another, which I recently wrote down in my journal: "Help me be more comfortable with being uncomfortable."

I mentioned earlier that we need to guard against making an idol out of our own comfort, but I want to take that a step further. See, I've learned that we actually need to embrace and welcome discomfort. I truly believe that. We make so much of our lives about avoiding discomfort, but discomfort can be a gift. When we are uncomfortable, we're forced to admit that we can't do it on our own. We're forced to rely on someone else. We're forced to grow. Comfort breeds complacency. Discomfort often leads to innovation and advancement—especially on the spiritual front.

"God chooses for you to be weak to protect you from you and to cause you to value the strength that only he can give," Tripp writes.[†]

I couldn't have said it better myself. Let's embrace the weakness (and the strength) found in being uncomfortable.

How do you think your discomfort could actually help you?

_____

_____

_____

_____

_____

_____

* There's a second part of this phrase that is equally important: "It's not OK to stay that way." We can recognize that we are struggling, but we need to be doing what we can (with God's help) to move forward.
† Tripp, *New Morning Mercies*, April 9.

What does it mean to you to boast in your weaknesses?

_____

_____

_____

_____

_____

The hymn "How Deep the Father's Love for Us" talks about boasting in Jesus Christ's death and resurrection. That's really short for: The only thing we can boast about is something we didn't even do, so we can't boast at all. What kind of comfort does that give you?

_____

_____

_____

_____

_____

_____

How do you think your struggle can actually bring God glory?

_____

_____

_____

_____

_____

 Make sure to read chapter 8 of *Finding Rest* before answering the following questions.

Chapter Questions

I find more rest by realizing my limitations than I do in pretending I have none. There's a difference between rest and forgetfulness. (Finding Rest, p. 142)

What do you think the difference is between finding rest and trying to forget about your struggle?

How can you come to terms with the fact that your anxiety is something you may have to continually fight without letting it define who you are?

How do you think that concept has had an effect on how you've approached your mental health?

My issues—your issues—come up again and again. And again. That's not meant to discourage you. It's meant to encourage you. It's normal. You are not broken beyond repair just because after experiencing a season on the mountaintop you find yourself in one of the deepest valleys. Maybe one day you will stay on top of that mountain. I hope so. But until then, understand that this is an ongoing battle. (*Finding Rest*, p. 139)

How can the idea that this may be an ongoing battle for you actually be an encouragement?

_____

_____

_____

_____

There certainly are times when I, as someone with anxiety and OCD, get laser-focused on something small and I obsess about it and it takes over. But I've also realized that I can tend to get caught up in the bigger picture. What I mean is that sometimes the goal of being "free" from my disorder becomes so overpowering that I lose sight of the small steps, the day-by-day wins, and the little victories. . . .

In other words, part of the ongoing battle of anxiety and OCD for me has been learning to focus on the smaller picture. (*Finding Rest*, p. 142)

What are some of the ways you personally can get caught up in the bigger picture?

_____

_____

_____

_____

Think about a recent time when you got caught in an anxious, or OCD, thought cycle. How could focusing on the smaller picture, or smaller steps, have helped you?

_____

_____

_____

_____

If you've had anxiety for any length of time, you've experienced the question that drives the ongoing battle. It's a question that leads to frantic thoughts and frenetic actions. A question that contains a lot of fear, especially for being only six letters long. That question is, "What if?" . . .

I call it the tyranny of the "What if?" (*Finding Rest*, pp. 144–45)

What are some of the "What if?" questions and worries that have typically haunted you?

> We anxiety sufferers have an inordinate fear of what *might* happen. We run through numerous possibilities in our heads until we grab hold of one that seems plausible (even if ridiculous) to us, and then we replay it over and over and over again. But by asking ourselves, "So what?" we strip the "What if?" of its power. The "So what?" forces us to think a little more rationally, a little more logically. (*Finding Rest*, p. 145)

Even if you haven't specifically adopted the "So what?" mantra, there are times in your past where you have overcome the tyranny of the "What if?" What has that looked like for you?

What is one way you can practically apply the idea of "So what?" to your anxiety and your anxious episodes?

Take action

In this chapter, we talked about the tyranny of the "What if?" It's the ever-present question for the anxiety sufferer. I was recently reminded of a song by singer-songwriter JJ Heller, titled none other than "God Is Still Here." In it, she details a lot of the "What if?" questions that she struggles with, but then she does something I absolutely love. She answers them with another question: "What if God is still here in this desert too?" That's very similar to the idea of answering the "What if?" questions with "So what?"

So here's what I want you to do: Use the table below to write your "What if?" questions in one column, and then in the column beside it write the "What if?" questions that are based on what you know to be true, what God has told you to be true. I'll give an example using my own struggle.

What if? (the lies)	What if? (the truth)
What if I struggle with worry, anxiety, or doubt for my entire life and can't handle it?	What if God has given me everything I need to make it through, no matter how long it lasts?

Pray

It's OK to pray that God will take away your suffering. You *should* do that. But if He doesn't, continue to pray that He will reveal what He wants you to learn and what He's doing to refine you. In fact, can I be so bold as to ask you to *thank* Him for it? There's something powerful that happens when we offer gratitude.

Example:

> *Father, I ask You now that You would take this cup from me. I know You can. Still, not my will, but Your will be done. Holy Spirit, whether this disease is taken from me or not, I ask that You would sustain me. I ask that You would show me how I can actually be grateful for what You are doing in and through this season—no matter how long the season lasts. Amen.*

For friends and family

The idea that this is an ongoing battle may be comforting for your loved one, but it may cause a lot of, well, anxiety in you. Write a prayer asking God to sustain *you* through this time, however long it lasts. Ask that He show you how He is using your loved one's struggle to refine and redefine *you* as well.

Write

Use this space to jot down any other thoughts that you may have about chapter 8.

LESSON 9

HELP ME UNDERSTAND

I HAVE A SPECIAL AFFINITY for this chapter in *Finding Rest*. It has become a breakout star and is thus the chapter I've gotten the most feedback on. I think that's because, even more than I realized when I first wrote it, this topic affects loved ones.

That makes sense if you think about it. For every individual with an anxiety or other mental health struggle, there are numerous other people in that person's sphere who are affected.

As a result, this chapter of the workbook is going to be a little different. Some questions will be for the sufferer who is reading these words, some for the loved one navigating these pages, and others for both. Answer the ones that relate to you and your situation.

⌒

I hate the pressure.

That's the word I use a lot to describe, somewhat inadequately, my anxiety: *pressure*.

If you're a sufferer I think that will make sense. If you're not, let me try to help you.

Recently, my wife asked me out of the blue: "Why don't we memorize a chapter of the Bible together?"

I tensed up. My jaw tightened. My heart raced. Instantly I felt pressure. Not pressure from her but pressure in general. See, the thought of having to memorize an entire chapter of the Bible doesn't inspire in me the awe, wonder, beauty, pride, and majesty that I think it deserves. No, instead my mind goes to all the requirements.

How much time will I have to carve out?

How am I going to fit it in?

What if I can't do it?

Why is my wife bringing this up now?

When I fail—because I will fail—what will she think about me?

What does not wanting to do this say about me?

Am I a bad Christian?

"I'm not really good at memorizing Scripture," I told her. "I don't really want to do that."

She was frustrated: "Why?"

Searching for the words in the moment, the only ones I could come up with were, "Because I don't like feeling the pressure."

It was the best I could do at the time. If you're the loved one of a sufferer, maybe you're reading this right now and you've heard that word. Maybe a light bulb is going off. Or maybe you are the sufferer and you're reading this and saying, "Yes! That's exactly how I feel!" Welcome to both of you.

As anxiety sufferers, we tend to feel a lot of pressure. Admittedly, it's pressure we put on ourselves—or rather, pressure our brains put on us. But while that pressure is a false assumption, it's also a real feeling.

That may seem like an odd thing to say, but it's the best way I can sum up the idea of pressure in the anxiety sufferer.

When my wife brought up the idea of memorizing Scripture, I instantly felt pressure. I instantly felt all those feelings. They are very real feelings for me. I do feel that way.

And yet, those feelings are rooted in false assumptions. Of course my wife would give me grace. Of course she wouldn't be a taskmaster. Of course she's not going to think less of me. She just wants to be in spiritual fellowship with me, her husband.

But those aren't the truths I automatically meditate on, because my brain is wired to go to worst-case scenarios. Instantly.

Here's the good news, though. Because of my experience with my disorder, while I may not have the best reactions in the moment, I've gotten to a place where I can take a step back and reevaluate my initial reactions and root out the lies. Funny enough, I do that a lot when I write.*

I tell you all that for two reasons. First, I want to help any loved ones of people like me understand why what you might consider a very benign suggestion (like studying Scripture) can cause a subpar reaction from those of us with anxiety disorders. It's because our minds can take the most innocent of suggestions and immediately feel pressure. Think of it like an imaginary voice changer that you're speaking into, turning something innocent into something pressure-inducing.

---

* I tell my wife regularly that "I think through my fingers." Sometimes when we get in an argument, I'll actually type up an email to her with my thoughts and response, because doing so allows me to be more clearheaded, cogent, and reasonable. It's a way I've found to fight back against my disorder. In fact, there are times she'll read an article of mine and facetiously say, "So *that's* what you were thinking."

That's why many anxiety sufferers avoid social situations. Those situations come with pressure—pressure to perform, pressure to please, pressure to be funny, pressure to be engaging, pressure to put on a face, pressure to remember names. Pressure, pressure, pressure. And remember, anxiety is an overactive fight-or-flight response, so when we feel such pressure, we tend to either run from it or fight back against it.

I hate that pressure. I wish I didn't feel it. But it is more of a companion in my life than I'd like it to be. And while I'm working on not bowing to the pressure, I'm not going to pretend it doesn't win from time to time. But I've found that the more I admit and talk about it to those I love, the easier it becomes to beat it.

The second reason I tell you all this is because I've realized that by vocalizing this phenomenon, the ones I love the most—and who are affected most by my feelings of pressure—can help me recognize it and move past it quicker.

Part of that involves what I call pressure release valves. That's exactly what a lot of the physical tools I talk about are. The best example for me? Running. If the pressure I feel creates a fight-or-flight response, I've found that physically fleeing (running) is helpful. It gets the angst out. It lets the pressure escape.

I encourage you to find those pressure release valves. And I pray this chapter in the workbook helps you do that.

Key Takeaways
- Anxiety, depression, or any other mental health struggle doesn't just affect the sufferer.
- There are aspects of anxiety that can actually be helpful and even lifesaving.
- Any response to a person with anxiety is best given after a relationship has been built.

Scripture
Two are better than one, because they have a good reward for their toil. For if they fall, one will lift up his fellow. But woe to him who is alone when he falls and has not another to lift him up! Again, if two lie together, they keep warm, but how can one keep warm alone? And though a man might prevail against one who is alone, two will withstand him—a threefold cord is not quickly broken. (Eccl. 4:9–12)

Philip ran to him and heard him reading Isaiah the prophet and asked, "Do you understand what you are reading?" And he said, "How can I, unless someone guides me?" And he invited Philip to come up and sit with him. . . . Then Philip opened his mouth, and beginning with this Scripture he told him the good news about Jesus. And as they were going along the road they came to some water, and the eunuch said, "See, here is water! What prevents me from being baptized?" And he commanded the chariot to stop, and they both went down into the water, Philip and the eunuch, and he baptized him. And when they came up out of the water, the Spirit of the Lord carried Philip away, and the eunuch saw him no more, and went on his way rejoicing. (Acts 8:30–31, 35–39)

These verses from Acts above have become some of my favorites. In the story, we see an influential Ethiopian trying his hardest to understand the Scriptures. That's when the Lord showed up, providing Philip as a means to help him. And the rest, as they say, is history.

Why do I love this story so much? Because it shows (1) that God honors our intentions to learn, grow, and understand Him better, even if it doesn't make sense to us in the moment; and (2) God uses our friends, family, or even strangers to help us understand Him better. That's what this chapter is all about. It's about gaining a deeper understanding of the struggle and how God can use friends, family members, loved ones, and even strangers (me?) in His work.

If you're a friend or family member, you can be used by God. If you're an anxiety sufferer, God can use others to help you, and He can use you to help others understand how He is at work amid your mental health struggles. It's a beautiful, multifaceted story that shows us exactly how God can work.

Maybe you're the Ethiopian in the story, or maybe you're Philip. Or maybe you switch between the two. That's OK. Whichever one you are, remember that God is using both the circumstances and you.

Looking back on your life, write about a time when God used you to illuminate who He is to others.

_____

_____

_____

_____

_____

_____

_____

_____

Now write about a time when God used someone else to help you understand Him better.

_____

_____

_____

_____

_____

 Make sure to read chapter 9 of *Finding Rest* before answering the following questions.

Chapter Questions

As much as I needed to name what was going on inside of me so I could understand it, Brett and those around me needed me to name it so they could start understanding me as well. (*Finding Rest*, p. 149)

How has your loved one's naming his or her disorder been helpful? Or how has that not happening made things more difficult?

_____

_____

_____

_____

_____

As someone who struggles with mental health, what do you wish your loved ones understood better?

_____

_____

_____

_____

_____

As a loved one of someone with a mental health challenge, what do you wish that person understood better about how his or her struggle affects you?

_____

_____

_____

_____

In order to understand anxiety, you have to realize that psychologically the person suffering from it is craving safety. That's because an anxiety disorder is the result of your brain not reacting correctly to fight-or-flight signals. (*Finding Rest*, p. 150)

Does this description help you understand your loved one's battle better? Why or why not?

_____

_____

_____

_____

The other thing that's important to understand about anxiety sufferers is that once we do move on from one fear, we are quick to find another. I can't tell you how many times I've laid in bed at night after a good, peaceful, restful day only to have my mind start searching for something to be wrong. (*Finding Rest*, p. 151)

If you struggle with anxiety, how has the above phenomenon affected your rest? If you are a loved one, how have you seen this play out?

_____

_____

_____

_____

_____

The seven deadly sins are all an excess of something good. In other words, they are an abnormal amount of something originally meant to be helpful, useful, and necessary. (*Finding Rest*, p. 152)

What has an excess of good anxiety (or self-preservation) looked like in your own life and relationships?

_____

_____

_____

_____

_____

Is it hard for you to see or understand how anxiety can actually be a good thing? Why or why not?

_____

_____

_____

_____

What are some ways your anxiety has manifested in healthy ways? (Or, for the loved one, what has healthy anxiety—or self-preservation—looked like in your friend or family member?)

_____

_____

_____

_____

What are some ways you have seen your anxiety actually help you in the past?

_____

_____

_____

_____

As a loved one, what are some phrases you've said in the past that you realize now may be unhelpful or even harmful?

_____

_____

_____

_____

_____

If you are someone who struggles, what words or phrases act as triggers for you?

_____

_____

_____

_____

Instead, what we need is for you to be *with* us instead of trying to *fix* us. We need you to talk *with* us instead of talking *at* us. One of the greatest weapons against anxiety is quality time spent with people who care. I'm not going to say it's like kryptonite. That's too immediate. It's more like an antibiotic: it needs to be taken regularly to get the full effects. (*Finding Rest*, p. 160)

Give a real-world example of talking *at* versus talking *with*.

_____

_____

_____

_____

That's what [my friend] Dan asks his wife. When he's struggling with something, he asks her if it's "real or not real" (or some variation), and she tells him the truth. It's a beautiful and concrete example of how she's earned the right to speak truth into his life, and how Dan relies on her to help him through the struggles. It also cuts to the core of his anxiety, since we sufferers have a hard time deciding between the real and the not-real threats. (*Finding Rest*, pp. 163–64)

How can you, as a loved one, balance calling out lies while also validating the real feelings that anxiety causes?

_____

_____

_____

_____

> I want to make it abundantly clear that as a family member or friend of someone with anxiety or OCD, you have the right to be heard too. (*Finding Rest*, p. 167)

As a loved one, how should you best communicate your feelings and what you're going through to your friend or family member?

_____

_____

_____

_____

As a sufferer, how can you best cultivate an environment where your friends or family members can be honest about what they're going through as well?

_____

_____

_____

_____

Take action

While this chapter in *Finding Rest* is practical (complete with a chart on what to say and what not to say), the only way any of it can be put into practice is to cultivate a relationship. The best way to do that is through honest, and sometimes tough, conversations. I want you to have one of those conversations.

Pick a time to sit down with the person or people in your life who are closest to you. If you are the sufferer, start by talking about what anxiety is like for you, and then work to convey what is most helpful for you in times of struggle. If you are a family member, open up about how this struggle has affected you, what you need in order to find rest, and also what you may want to improve at as you move forward. Then come to a genuine understanding of what going forward can look like based on the truths in this chapter. For both of you, own past mistakes. Be honest about any struggles. Strive to give the other person the benefit of the doubt. Then pray together that the Holy Spirit will help you on this journey of understanding.

Pray

Whether you are the sufferer or the loved one, pray for grace and understanding.
   Example:

> *Jesus, thank You that You offered us grace. Thank You that You completely under-stand what I'm going through, even when I can't fully convey it. Holy Spirit, give me empathy as we cultivate a relationship built on truth and grace. Let all my words be soaked in who You are and what You are about. Convict me where I need to be convicted, and give me boldness to talk about hard things. Amen.*

For friends and family

Let's talk about pressure release valves. This concept is an important one. There's a reason the phrase "blowing off steam" is popular. The saying comes from the railroad industry, at a time when steam engines powered locomotives. Back then, there were no safety valves, so if too much steam built up, the engine would simply explode. To prevent that, the conductor would release the pressure by opening up a valve and then quite literally blow off the excess steam.

   We all need pressure release valves. For an anxiety sufferer especially, the pressure (as I talked about earlier) can build faster and more violently. The exercise I just detailed above is a way to release that pressure. However, I want you to think about the idea of being a pressure release valve, and write out three practical ways (besides deep one-on-one conversation) that can accomplish this. Maybe it's scheduling regular movie nights, date nights, or something similar. Whatever it is, make it personal.

_____

_____

_____

_____

_____

_____

Write

Use this space to jot down any other thoughts that you may have about chapter 9.

L E S S O N   1 0

THE FOURTEEN TRUTHS

BECAUSE THE WORKBOOK FOLLOWS THE format of *Finding Rest*, this specific section will be more extensive than previous chapters. But while it is longer, I still want you to take your time and really meditate on how each one of these truths affects you. Don't rush through them.

⌐

For much of my life I struggled with prayer.

When I talk about treating God like a vending machine, I say that based on experience. That's what prayer traditionally was for me. I thought if I put the money in, followed all the steps, I could pick what I got out. And if what I prayed for didn't happen, there was something wrong with what I was putting into the machine. Maybe I didn't have the proper change, maybe the change was too dirty, or maybe the change was fake. Whatever the problem was, my goal was to find the magical combination so I could unlock God and get Him to give me what I wanted.

"Your father owns the cattle on a thousand hills," my parents used to say. "All you have to do is tap into that power."

That's true . . . to a certain extent. But it's not the full truth. The Bible does say that God owns the cattle on a thousand hills, but that statement isn't about tapping into His power and riches. Here's the passage from Psalm 50:7–15:

> Hear, O my people, and I will speak;
>   O Israel, I will testify against you.
>   I am God, your God.
> Not for your sacrifices do I rebuke you;

your burnt offerings are continually before me.
I will not accept a bull from your house
 or goats from your folds.
For every beast of the forest is mine,
 the cattle on a thousand hills.
I know all the birds of the hills,
 and all that moves in the field is mine.

If I were hungry, I would not tell you,
 for the world and its fullness are mine.
Do I eat the flesh of bulls
 or drink the blood of goats?
Offer to God a sacrifice of thanksgiving,
 and perform your vows to the Most High,
and call upon me in the day of trouble;
 I will deliver you, and you shall glorify me.

Essentially, God is telling His people that He's tired of having their physical sacrifices but not their hearts. He doesn't care about goats or bulls because He has so many of them already! The point of a sacrifice isn't to offer a physical animal; the point is to orient our hearts. It isn't about the stuff, and it's certainly not about trying to curry favor with God.

Just listen to how the *ESV Study Bible* sums up Psalm 50:

> The God who speaks and summons the earth (v. 1) especially plans to judge his own people (v. 4), particularly to warn any of them who presume on the privileges of the sacrificial system thinking that it is a way to buy God off, apart from a living relationship with him.[*]

Psalm 50 isn't about using prayer to "tap into God's power" and riches (as suggested to me during my upbringing). In fact, it's the opposite! It's God *warning* us not to try to curry His favor and instead give Him the most important sacrifice we have: our hearts.

So what's my point? Context matters, especially in these verses. But too many times we take one verse and apply it to something it wasn't meant to be applied to and then turn it into a universal truth. This is what I call coffee-cup Christianity.

We do this with another popular verse, Philippians 4:13, as well: "I can do all things through him who strengthens me." How many of us have heard this verse used to

---

[*] *ESV Study Bible* (Wheaton, IL: Crossway, 2008), 998.

explain that we can do anything we want because we have God on our side? (I'm raising my hand really high right now.)

But do you know what the context of that verse is? It's actually Paul talking about how he's learned to be content amid his troubles. He's not using it as a motivational tool to run through a wall, but rather as an explanation of how he's been able to endure the highs and lows of the past and in the future. Here's Philippians 4:10–13 for full context:

> I rejoiced in the Lord greatly that now at length you have revived your concern for me. You were indeed concerned for me, but you had no opportunity. Not that I am speaking of being in need, for I have learned in whatever situation I am to be content. I know how to be brought low, and I know how to abound. In any and every circumstance, I have learned the secret of facing plenty and hunger, abundance and need. I can do all things through him who strengthens me.

In other words, this isn't some feel-good verse about conquering anything in your way. Rather, it's a verse to explain how to be content when those obstacles *remain* in your way. Context matters.[*]

Why do I say all this as an introduction to a chapter about the truths we need to embrace? Because we have to have a true hunger for truth—the full truth, not half-truths or just truths that make us feel better, and certainly not the truths of coffee-cup Christianity. The truths of this chapter are rooted in Scripture (although they are not all spiritual). As you meditate on them, keep that in mind. Test them against Scripture. Test them against who we know God is.

When it comes to prayer, then, I want you to realize that there is so much more to prayer than getting what you want. I struggled with prayer for so long because that's how I treated it. But sometimes the point is that you actually *don't* get what you *think* you want.[†] That's why it can't be reduced to our desires. Instead, it's an essential part of our relationship with our Creator. Bringing to light the truths contained in this chapter of *Finding Rest* was only made possible by my changing my perception of prayer and actually spending time with God because He's God, not because He's a vending machine.

I pray that your own relationship with God will be enriched by a proper understanding of prayer, and that even greater truths are revealed to you. Truths that are so much better, deeper, and richer than what can fit on a coffee cup.

---

* By the way, a new coffee cup has popped up as a result of people realizing this verse has been taken out of context. It says something like this: "I can do all things through a verse taken out of context." Now *that's* a mug I want!

† I often like to say that Garth Brooks is an accidental theologian with his song "Unanswered Prayers."

Key Takeaways

- Your anxiety or other mental health struggle is not God punishing you.
- You are broken. I am broken. We all are broken, whether we have anxiety or not.
- Shame can make our battle seem hopeless, but it is not.

Scripture

Finally, brothers, whatever is true, whatever is honorable, whatever is just, whatever is pure, whatever is lovely, whatever is commendable, if there is any excellence, if there is anything worthy of praise, think about these things. (Phil. 4:8)

This verse is another one that has been weaponized against a lot of us anxiety sufferers. The idea goes something like this, "I know you're anxious and worried, but the Bible says to just think about good things. So do that."

You and I both know that if it were that easy, we would not need this book or workbook. Yet while I don't want to ignore how coffee-cup Christianity has been harmful to you, I do want to encourage you to look past how this verse may have been used against you in the past and see the deep truths in it.

While I simply can't turn my stressful thoughts off like a faucet, I have found that the more I fill my mind with things that are honorable, just, pure, lovely, commendable, excellent, and worthy of praise, the clearer my mind becomes. So here's my encouragement to you: Instead of using this verse in times of emergency, use it to prepare and cultivate your mind to help prevent more of those emergency situations. Think of it as that daily baby aspirin to prevent heart blockages instead of a defibrillator to restart your heart. That's been an encouraging way for me to look at it, and I think it will be for you too.

What is one way you can better practice thinking about what is "pure and lovely" to prepare you to do battle during an anxious episode?

_____

_____

_____

_____

_____

_____

What role does prayer play in your life? What's one thing you can do to improve that?

_____

_____

_____

_____

 Make sure to read chapter 10 of *Finding Rest* before answering the following questions.

Chapter Questions

Before you go any further, list the three truths that resonated with you most.

_____

_____

_____

_____

Now I want to take you through each truth. Again, be sure to spend time thinking through each one, and avoid rushing.

1. For Your Good and His Glory

When you accept and internalize that God is using your struggles for good, you're forced to accept the larger truth that God is *also* good. If He's using your *struggles* for good, you have to accept that *He* is good too. (A bad God can't produce good things.) (*Finding Rest*, p. 171)

Why is it essential to understand and accept that God is good in order to grasp this truth?

_____

_____

_____

_____

Sometimes the very thing we fear the most, the very thing we're running from, is exactly what a loving God is using to refine us, to draw us to Himself, and even to restore our relationships. (*Finding Rest*, p. 171)

How have you seen evidence that God has used the very thing you fear to draw you to Him?

_____

_____

_____

_____

If you haven't, how can you prepare yourself so that your reaction is like Paul's in Philippians 4:13?

_____

_____

_____

_____

_____

2. You Have a Pride Issue

What was your initial reaction to hearing that anxiety is fueled by pride?

_____

_____

_____

_____

_____

Baked into the foundation of our anxiety are three types of lies. First, we can figure things out on our own (we don't need God). Second, we're smarter than God (we think what He says to be true isn't *really* true). Third, if we try hard enough, we can make anything work (we're stronger than God). At the heart of all those is this idea that we are superior and don't need His help. (*Finding Rest*, p. 172)

Which one of the above lies has been most prominent in your life?

What's one practical way you can work on giving up control this week?

---

3. God Isn't Punishing You

Your anxiety, your OCD, your depression, your whatever else are not punishments for sin in your life. God is not examining your ledger from last weekend and doling out a little anxiety here or a little depression there to make you pay for your bad word, lustful thought, or shameful comment. That's not how this works. (*Finding Rest*, p. 172)

What would you say to someone who suggests that your struggle is punishment?

When someone says "God," what image comes to mind? Write it down.

_____

_____

_____

_____

_____

Our image and conception of God can be severely influenced by our past. For those who had an absent or abusive dad, for example, the idea of God as a loving Father can be hard to grasp. Write down some of the things from your past that may have hindered you from viewing God as a loving Father, a comforter, or even a powerful protector.

_____

_____

_____

_____

_____

4. You Are Broken

> Friend, your legs are broken. My legs are broken. Our minds are weak. And only God can ultimately heal us, take care of us, and lead us to rest. (*Finding Rest*, pp. 173–74)

Why is there freedom in accepting our brokenness?

_____

_____

_____

_____

_____

How can you boast in your weakness while simultaneously guarding against being complacent about where you are?

----

5. *There Is Hope*

Shame is one of those tiny tools the devil uses to drive a wedge between us and the One who loves us most. When we feel shame, we retreat. When we retreat, we hide. When we hide, we surrender the one thing that can get rid of the shame: intimacy with God. (*Finding Rest*, p. 175)

Have you suffered feelings of shame in your life, maybe as a result of your disorder or the actions your disorder has led you to take? If so, describe it here.

How would you describe the difference between shame and remorse?

Maybe you've heard this before, but it's worth repeating. It's worth burning it into the forefront of your mind and meditating on during those times when your enemy convinces you to give up hope: sometimes we feel like God is digging a grave, but He's really digging a well. (*Finding Rest*, p. 175)

What does "Sometimes we feel like God is digging a grave, but He's really digging a well" mean to you?

What is one way you've felt God was digging a grave for you only to realize He was really digging a well?

---

6. Embrace Tiny Victories

If you're like me (if you're reading this book, you are like me or know someone who is), your anxiety and OCD tell you a lot of lies. One of those lies is that you should be doing more than you're doing or you should have done more than you did. (*Finding Rest*, p. 175)

What are some of the lies that your disorder tells you, lies you struggle fighting against?

When you're climbing out of a crevice, the wisest thing to do is focus on the step immediately in front of you instead of the seemingly insurmountable wall above you. (*Finding Rest*, p. 176)

What are some of the tiny victories you can focus on the next time you face an anxious episode?

_____

_____

_____

_____

_____

7. Medication Is OK

It is not wrong. It is not an admission of defeat. It is not a sin to take medication for your mental health struggles. (*Finding Rest*, p. 176)

Based on what you've read in the book, how is taking medication not an admission of defeat?

_____

_____

_____

_____

_____

Have your thoughts about medication changed at all as a result of reading this? If so, how? If not, why?

_____

_____

_____

_____

_____

_____

How would you describe common grace to someone else?

_____

_____

_____

_____

8. *It's an Ongoing Battle*

> I can simultaneously still struggle while also finding some semblance of rest. It's a paradox. I live—we live—in that paradox. And that's OK.
> It's the reality of life this side of heaven. (*Finding Rest*, p. 177)

How would you describe the "paradox" of struggling while also finding rest?

_____

_____

_____

_____

How does it make you feel to think that your mental health struggle could be something you face the rest of your life?

_____

_____

_____

_____

_____

Write out what you've come to understand is a proper theology of suffering.

_____

_____

_____

_____

9. *It's Never Too Late*

It is never too late to fight back against what's going on inside of you. It's never too late to take care of yourself. It's never too late to throw yourself into the arms of Jesus. (*Finding Rest*, p. 177)

When has your disorder made you feel the most hopeless?

_____

_____

_____

_____

What gives you the most hope going forward?

_____

_____

_____

_____

What does it look like in your life to fight back? List three practical ways.

_____

_____

_____

_____

10. *You Need Community*

From the beginning of time we have been trained to hide when we feel shame. Just look at Adam and Eve. But our wounds can only be healed when they are exposed to the light, and many times we need others to rip off the Band-Aids. (*Finding Rest*, p. 178)

Who are the people in your life you can turn to when you need support?

_____

_____

_____

_____

What can you do to build trust among your friends and community, so that if and when they have to give you some hard truth, you do not get defensive?

_____

_____

_____

_____

Is there anything you've been hiding from your friends or community for fear of what they'd think or because it's embarrassing? If so, write it down and then pray for the courage to share it.

_____

_____

_____

_____

11. Your Struggle Doesn't Affect Just You

I said earlier that our anxiety and our depression can be inherently selfish. That wasn't a typo. In every sense of the word, both those things at their worst are overwhelmingly self-focused. They both lead to perpetual navel-gazing. (*Finding Rest*, p. 180)

Who are the people in your life who have been affected most by your disorder?

_____

_____

_____

_____

What are some evidences of your being too self-focused—even when due to your disorder—that you can be on the lookout for?

_____

_____

_____

_____

How can you better practice giving grace as freely as you'd like to receive it?

_____

_____

_____

_____

12. Help Others

If you feel stuck in an episode, make a conscious effort to sacrifice for someone else. It changes your gaze and your mindset, and can be a gateway to relief. (*Finding Rest*, p. 181)

Why do you think serving others can be good for breaking out of an anxious thought episode?

_____

_____

_____

_____

List two things you can do this week to serve others.

_____

_____

_____

_____

13. *God Can Handle Your Anger*

As Christians, we do this thing where we forget how ordinary some of the Bible's most prominent figures are. Do you know what ordinary people do? They get angry, and they get angry at God. (*Finding Rest*, p. 181)

Have you ever been angry at God? Describe that time.

How does it help to humanize some of the prominent figures in the Bible?

Write out a statement of lament for what's going on in your life right now.

---

14. *Take Care of Yourself*

One of the most important lessons I hope you glean from these pages is that what's going on inside of you at this moment—the fears, the thoughts, the despair—is mental, physical, *and* spiritual. The best way to take care of your mental health is through a regimen that addresses the three facets of it: brain, body, and spirit. That means you need to invest in spiritual remedies as well as physical and psychological ones. Medication can be one of those physical remedies. But there are others: exercise, diet, and rest are just a few. (*Finding Rest*, p. 182)

What are three ways you can commit to taking care of yourself spiritually?

_____

_____

_____

What are three ways you can commit to taking care of yourself physically?

_____

_____

_____

Take action

Earlier, I asked you to list the three truths that resonated with you the most. Now I want you to whittle that down to the one truth you need the most right now. The key words are "right now." It's OK that different truths will resonate with you at different times. Once you have picked your one truth for now, write down one practical way this week that you can put it into practice.

Pray

The Holy Spirit has been sent as a helper. Ask the Holy Spirit to guide you daily, convict you often, and lead you toward more truths that affect your heart.

Example:

> *Holy Spirit, thank You for being my daily helper. Thank You also for illuminating God's truth to me. I ask that You continue to do so. Show me where I haven't fully trusted You, guide me toward a deeper understanding of the Father and the Son, and help me grow to be more like Christ. Amen.*

For friends and family

What are some truths you've come to understand as a result of reading *Finding Rest*? Write them out, and then add a practical way you can put them into practice.

_____

_____

_____

Write

Use this space to jot down any other thoughts that you may have about chapter 10.

E P I L O G U E

I WANT TO TALK TO you about my favorite hymn of all time and how its words became true for me. Why? Because it's the culmination of everything I have learned, experienced, and prayed for, and it's my prayer for you.

This hymn is not my favorite just because of the lyrics, although they are incredible. It's not my favorite because of the melody, although it is soothing. No, the biggest reason it is my favorite hymn is because of the story behind it. The words, the melody, and the message are so much more powerful as a result.

That story centers around the hymn's author, Horatio Spafford. Maybe you're familiar with the general story, but I want to go deeper. Spafford reminds me of Job.

Spafford and his wife, Anna, had five children just before the turn of the last century. Four girls—Annie, Maggie, Bessie, and Tanetta—and one boy, Horatio Jr. In 1870, however, the young son died of scarlet fever. Horatio and Anna were devastated. But they would come to know even greater pain than that.

In 1871, the Spaffords lost most of their successful law practice in the Great Chicago Fire. Their livelihood literally went up in flames. But they would come to know even greater pain than that.

Sounding familiar? Sounding Job-esque?

Two years later, the Spaffords had planned a trip to Europe, in part to help the legendary evangelist D. L. Moody. As the family got ready to embark, though, a business emergency came up. So Horatio sent Anna and the four girls ahead of him on the ship, with plans to catch another one a few days later.

But again tragedy struck.

The ship Anna and the girls were on collided with another boat in the middle of the Atlantic Ocean. Within twelve minutes it sank, and all four of the young Spafford girls died. Anna barely survived and was only saved by a small rowboat after literally holding on for dear life to a piece of driftwood.

After Horatio got the news, he packed his things and left to be with his wife. A few days into his trip, the captain alerted him that they were passing over the exact spot where his daughters had perished. It was at that time that Spafford stared down and penned these amazing words that we've come to know as the hymn, "It Is Well with My Soul":

When peace like a river attendeth my way
When sorrows like sea billows roll
Whatever my lot, Thou hast taught me to say
It is well, it is well with my soul

Chorus:
It is well
With my soul
It is well, it is well with my soul

Though Satan should buffet, though trials should come
Let this blest assurance control
That Christ has regarded my helpless estate
And has shed His own blood for my soul

(Chorus)

My sin, oh the bliss of this glorious thought
My sin, not in part, but the whole
Is nailed to the cross, and I bear it no more
Praise the Lord, praise the Lord, O my soul

(Chorus)

And Lord, haste the day when my faith shall be sight
The clouds be rolled back as a scroll
The trump shall resound, and the Lord shall descend
Even so, it is well with my soul

(Chorus)

So much truth sandwiched between so much tragedy. Can you see now why it's my favorite hymn? To go through all Horatio Spafford did and yet still pen those words is absolutely incredible. Spafford knew immense suffering. He knew what it was like to lose. He knew pain intimately. Yet through it all, he resolved, "It is well with my soul."*

That, friends, is a proper theology of suffering. That is not judging God by your circumstances but, rather, judging your circumstances by who you know God is. But while I've said for years how much I love those words and love that story, I never expected to be on the precipice of experiencing what Spafford experienced. In 2022, though, I was.

Early in the spring, as I was writing this workbook, something odd started happening with my four-year-old son. One day as my wife and I were watching him play, we noticed he was limping. It wasn't as if he had broken an ankle, but it was an obvious "hitch in his giddyup," as they say here in Texas.

My wife and I chalked it up to growing pains. However, as the days went by, it got progressively worse. Eventually it led to his waking up nearly every night with severe leg pain. He would come into our room and beg us to rub his leg to make it go away, sometimes moaning as he drifted off into restless sleep.

After a couple weeks of this routine, we took him to an orthopedic doctor to get X-rays. The doctor told us he couldn't find anything abnormal, and we should simply monitor it. Then he sent us on our way.

It didn't stop, though.

Neither my son nor us (and especially my wife) were getting any sleep. His daycare even told us he was complaining about constant pain during the day. A few months into the ordeal, we took him back to the doctor for more X-rays to try to figure it out. This time, though, the physician noticed something odd.

"You need to take him to his pediatrician right away," he said, after seeing abnormal thickening near the top of his shinbone.

We rushed to the pediatrician that same day, with plenty of scenarios playing out in our heads. But the pediatrician at that appointment didn't take us seriously. He ordered some blood work, and when it came back normal, he wrote in his notes that he didn't think anything was wrong, citing the fact that my son, although in immense pain, was quite literally bouncing off the walls during the exam.

We were confused, slightly angry, and worried. We did what you aren't supposed to do: we started googling his symptoms. As we did, we came up with two very clear options: a benign tumor or a cancerous one. The limp, the pain at night, and what the orthopedic doctor saw on the second X-ray all fit.

Discontent with the diagnosis (or lack thereof) from the pediatrician, and armed with the power of Google, my wife and I fought for an answer. We found a pediatric orthopedic specialist in the area and scheduled an appointment. That meeting went

---

* You can find more details about that ordeal, including Anna's account of the accident, in an article by Jane Winstead that's been archived here: http://www.postpresby.org/Audio%20Sermon%20Files/2010/Spafford.htm.

much differently. Immediately after looking at my son's X-rays and watching him walk, the specialist ordered an emergency MRI, which meant our getting up at 5:30 the next morning and having our son go under general anesthesia.

Within hours we had our answer, and it was one of the things we had feared. Our son had a tumor in his shin; which type, we didn't yet know.

It was a gut punch.

Before I go any further, let me say that I've always wondered what it would be like to have faith like Horatio Spafford. I always wondered what I would do if I was in a similar situation, and every time the story plays out in my mind it doesn't end with me writing an incredible hymn about the goodness of God and being content.

Yet in this season, that's exactly what happened (minus the writing-the-incredible-hymn part).

I remember my wife asking me what I was thinking one night as we sat in the living room talking through what we could be facing. I looked at her and, with a confidence I can't explain, said, "I just know that God's got us, no matter what happens."

Friend, God's got you. In this season, in the past seasons, and in the next season, He's got you. I know it may not seem like it. I know there are times you feel alone. But I'm telling you, God's got you.

The abyss of mental health can be a scary one to stare into. Not just because of the darkness but because of the shapes and images your mind populates when you look down. In some ways, the nothingness of just the darkness would be a relief.

But I'm here to tell you that when you draw near to God, there will come a time when He shows up in a way that makes no sense and that you can't explain. A time when all you can say, when staring into that hole, is, "It is well with my soul."

For years I have admired Horatio Spafford. I have begged God to give me his type of faith. What I didn't realize, though, is that for years that's exactly what He has been doing. For years He has been using my struggle to prepare me for moments just like this. For years He has been speaking to my spirit, shaping me, and molding me. For years He has been showing up.

"It is well with my soul" isn't a singular, momentary realization. It's an overnight epiphany years in the making. It just took this issue for me to see it.

I tell you this story not to build myself up or to show you how I've nailed it. I tell you this story to boast, like Paul, in my weakness.

Friend, I am an anxious person. You know that by now. And if you are too, then you know what generally *should* cause you anxiety. My son's condition should have caused me anxiety.

It didn't.

I can honestly say that, as I stared into an unknown diagnosis for my son in which cancer was on the table, God was with me.

That's my prayer for you. Not just that you would experience that same comfort but that you would also see how God is using your struggle, your hardship, your pain, to draw you to Him and show you how He has been working throughout your life, even when you didn't realize it.

If you put into practice what you've discovered about yourself, about God, and about the truths He's given us, as shared in these pages, I truly believe you can and will get to the point where it is well with your soul. It won't happen overnight, but I think you'll find that one day you're going to face an obstacle and be surprised at your perspective, just as I was.

So what about my son's diagnosis? We found out the tumor is benign, not cancerous. That determination came after a week of tests and more weeks of waiting that felt like being stuck at the DMV. But in an interesting way, God's power was most on display for me not in getting the ultimate diagnosis I prayed for. Rather, His power became evident to me long before, when I rode over the deep waters, stared down into the unknown, and said, "It is well with my soul."

That is rest. That is comfort. That is God.

And He's got you.

ACKNOWLEDGMENTS

IT TAKES MORE PEOPLE THAN you'd think to bring a project like this to fruition. The person who sacrifices the most deserves first mention here: my wife, Brett. Thank you for always being my cheerleader (even if you laugh every time you see that picture of me in high school with an actual cheerleader). I love you more than I can ever convey.

Second, I want to acknowledge you, the reader. This workbook would have never happened if you had not picked up *Finding Rest*, read it, and shared it with others. I cherish your emails, your social media posts and messages, and your support. I am honored and humbled you have, even in a small way, allowed me to give you a voice.

The friendships the Lord has blessed me with are too numerous to count, but I especially want to thank Tanner Stevenson and Ben Jordan. You both have continued to sharpen me, challenge me, and laugh with (and at) me. I can't thank God enough for you. You have shown me what true community and friendship look like.

The team at Kregel has been invaluable. Thank you, Catherine DeVries, for believing in me. To the editors, Ken Walker, Sarah De Mey, and Robert Hartig, I appreciate your patience—especially when you tell me I can't use song lyrics and I have to rewrite chapters because of that. You make me better.

Finally, thank you to my agent, Cyle Young, who continues to see how much the message in these pages is needed right now, and who has worked hard to see it amplified.

Thank you.

NOTES

NOTES

NOTES

NOTES

NOTES

NOTES

NOTES

NOTES

"If you are tired, beaten down, and looking for hope, these words will be water to your soul."

—MEGAN ALEXANDER, *Inside Edition* correspondent
and author of *Faith in the Spotlight*

FOREWORD BY KIRK CAMERON

FINDING REST

A Survivor's Guide
to Navigating the Valleys of
Anxiety, Faith, and Life

JONATHON M. SEIDL

"Jon knows better than most what it means to battle anxiety and how to forge a path to victory. He also treats it with care, and pushes the conversation to places that it hasn't often gone in the church."
—KIRK CAMERON

KREGEL
PUBLICATIONS